ISBN 0-8373-3368-7

C-3368   CAREER EXAMINATION SERIES

This is your
PASSBOOK® for...

Developmental Disabilities Program Specialist I

Test Preparation Study Guide
Questions & Answers

NATIONAL LEARNING CORPORATION

(516) 921-8888
(800) 645-6337
FAX: (516) 921-8743
www.passbooks.com
sales @ passbooks.com
info @ passbooks.com

PRINTED IN THE UNITED STATES OF AMERICA

PASSBOOK®

NOTICE

PASSBOOK® SERIES

THE *PASSBOOK® SERIES* has been created to prepare applicants and candidates for the ultimate academic battlefield – the examination room.

At some time in our lives, each and every one of us may be required to take an examination – for validation, matriculation, admission, qualification, registration, certification, or licensure.

Based on the assumption that every applicant or candidate has met the basic formal educational standards, has taken the required number of courses, and read the necessary texts, the *PASSBOOK® SERIES* furnishes the one special preparation which may assure passing with confidence, instead of failing with insecurity. Examination questions – together with answers – are furnished as the basic vehicle for study so that the mysteries of the examination and its compounding difficulties may be eliminated or diminished by a sure method.

This book is meant to help you pass your examination provided that you qualify and are serious in your objective.

The entire field is reviewed through the huge store of content information which is succinctly presented through a provocative and challenging approach – the question-and-answer method.

A climate of success is established by furnishing the correct answers at the end of each test.

You soon learn to recognize types of questions, forms of questions, and patterns of questioning. You may even begin to anticipate expected outcomes.

You perceive that many questions are repeated or adapted so that you can gain acute insights, which may enable you to score many sure points.

You learn how to confront new questions, or types of questions, and to attack them confidently and work out the correct answers.

You note objectives and emphases, and recognize pitfalls and dangers, so that you may make positive educational adjustments.

Moreover, you are kept fully informed in relation to new concepts, methods, practices, and directions in the field.

You discover that you are actually taking the examination all the time: you are preparing for the examination by "taking" an examination, not by reading extraneous and/or supererogatory textbooks.

In short, this PASSBOOK®, used directedly, should be an important factor in helping you to pass your test.

DEVELOPMENTAL DISABILITIES PROGRAM SPECIALIST I

DUTIES

As a Developmental Disabilities Program Specialist I, you would design and develop day services and community residential opportunities for individuals with mental retardation and developmental disabilities. You would assist local public and private agencies in identifying individuals eligible for services, in determining the needs and choices of consumers, and in identifying the services and settings best suited to meet these needs and choices. You would assist agencies with budget preparation, staffing plans, site development, and identification of funding sources. Some positions may require general supervisory responsibility.

SUBJECT OF EXAMINATION

The written test is designed to test for knowledge, skills, and/or abilities in such areas as:

1. **Preparing written material** - These questions test for the ability to present information clearly and accurately, and to organize paragraphs logically and comprehensibly. For some questions, you will be given information in two or three sentences followed by four restatements of the information. You must then choose the best version. For other questions, you will be given paragraphs with their sentences out of order and then asked to choose from four suggestions the best order for the sentences.

2. **Program planning and evaluation** - These questions test for a knowledge of basic concepts and techniques in such areas as the planning function, factors involved in implementing new procedures or programs, and evaluating their results and effectiveness. The questions are conceptual in approach and fundamental in level; they do not involve the manipulation of data nor the application of quantitative methods.

3. **Care and understanding of developmentally disabled individuals** - These questions test for knowledge and understanding of the characteristics and problems of developmentally disabled individuals and the habilitation practices and techniques used with such individuals. Questions may cover such topics as the symptoms, causes, prognoses, and habilitation techniques associated with various developmental disabilities; physical, psychological, intellectual, and social characteristics of developmentally disabled individuals; and habilitation and case management practices which promote the level of functioning of developmentally disabled individuals.

4. **Supervision** - These questions test for knowledge of the principles and practices employed in planning, organizing, and controlling the activities of a work unit toward predetermined objectives. They appropriately test for a first-line supervisory position. The concepts covered, usually in a situational question format, may include, but are not necessarily restricted to: assigning and reviewing work; evaluating performance; maintaining work standards; motivating and developing subordinates; implementing procedural change; increasing efficiency; and dealing with problems of absenteeism, morale and discipline.

5. **Understanding and interpreting written material** - These questions test how well you comprehend written material. You will be provided with brief reading selections and will be asked questions about the selections. All the information required to answer the questions will be presented in the selections; you will not be required to have any special knowledge relating to the subject areas of the selections.

HOW TO TAKE A TEST

I. YOU MUST PASS AN EXAMINATION

A. *WHAT EVERY CANDIDATE SHOULD KNOW*

Examination applicants often ask us for help in preparing for the written test. What can I study in advance? What kinds of questions will be asked? How will the test be given? How will the papers be graded?

As an applicant for a civil service examination, you may be wondering about some of these things. Our purpose here is to suggest effective methods of advance study and to describe civil service examinations.

Your chances for success on this examination can be increased if you know how to prepare. Those "pre-examination jitters" can be reduced if you know what to expect. You can even experience an adventure in good citizenship if you know why civil service exams are given.

B. *WHY ARE CIVIL SERVICE EXAMINATIONS GIVEN?*

Civil service examinations are important to you in two ways. As a citizen, you want public jobs filled by employees who know how to do their work. As a job seeker, you want a fair chance to compete for that job on an equal footing with other candidates. The best-known means of accomplishing this two-fold goal is the competitive examination.

Exams are widely publicized throughout the nation. They may be administered for jobs in federal, state, city, municipal, town or village governments or agencies.

Any citizen may apply, with some limitations, such as the age or residence of applicants. Your experience and education may be reviewed to see whether you meet the requirements for the particular examination. When these requirements exist, they are reasonable and applied consistently to all applicants. Thus, a competitive examination may cause you some uneasiness now, but it is your privilege and safeguard.

C. *HOW ARE CIVIL SERVICE EXAMS DEVELOPED?*

Examinations are carefully written by trained technicians who are specialists in the field known as "psychological measurement," in consultation with recognized authorities in the field of work that the test will cover. These experts recommend the subject matter areas or skills to be tested; only those knowledges or skills important to your success on the job are included. The most reliable books and source materials available are used as references. Together, the experts and technicians judge the difficulty level of the questions.

Test technicians know how to phrase questions so that the problem is clearly stated. Their ethics do not permit "trick" or "catch" questions. Questions may have been tried out on sample groups, or subjected to statistical analysis, to determine their usefulness.

Written tests are often used in combination with performance tests, ratings of training and experience, and oral interviews. All of these measures combine to form the best-known means of finding the right person for the right job.

II. HOW TO PASS THE WRITTEN TEST

A. NATURE OF THE EXAMINATION

To prepare intelligently for civil service examinations, you should know how they differ from school examinations you have taken. In school you were assigned certain definite pages to read or subjects to cover. The examination questions were quite detailed and usually emphasized memory. Civil service exams, on the other hand, try to discover your present ability to perform the duties of a position, plus your potentiality to learn these duties. In other words, a civil service exam attempts to predict how successful you will be. Questions cover such a broad area that they cannot be as minute and detailed as school exam questions.

In the public service similar kinds of work, or positions, are grouped together in one "class." This process is known as *position-classification*. All the positions in a class are paid according to the salary range for that class. One class title covers all of these positions, and they are all tested by the same examination.

B. FOUR BASIC STEPS

1) Study the announcement

How, then, can you know what subjects to study? Our best answer is: "Learn as much as possible about the class of positions for which you've applied." The exam will test the knowledge, skills and abilities needed to do the work.

Your most valuable source of information about the position you want is the official exam announcement. This announcement lists the training and experience qualifications. Check these standards and apply only if you come reasonably close to meeting them.

The brief description of the position in the examination announcement offers some clues to the subjects which will be tested. Think about the job itself. Review the duties in your mind. Can you perform them, or are there some in which you are rusty? Fill in the blank spots in your preparation.

Many jurisdictions preview the written test in the exam announcement by including a section called "Knowledge and Abilities Required," "Scope of the Examination," or some similar heading. Here you will find out specifically what fields will be tested.

2) Review your own background

Once you learn in general what the position is all about, and what you need to know to do the work, ask yourself which subjects you already know fairly well and which need improvement. You may wonder whether to concentrate on improving your strong areas or on building some background in your fields of weakness. When the announcement has specified "some knowledge" or "considerable knowledge," or has used adjectives like "beginning principles of..." or "advanced ... methods," you can get a clue as to the number and difficulty of questions to be asked in any given field. More questions, and hence broader coverage, would be included for those subjects which are more important in the work. Now weigh your strengths and weaknesses against the job requirements and prepare accordingly.

3) Determine the level of the position

Another way to tell how intensively you should prepare is to understand the level of the job for which you are applying. Is it the entering level? In other words, is this the position in which beginners in a field of work are hired? Or is it an intermediate or advanced level? Sometimes this is indicated by such words as "Junior" or "Senior" in the class title. Other jurisdictions use Roman numerals to designate the level – Clerk I, Clerk II, for example. The word "Supervisor" sometimes appears in the title. If the level is not indicated by the title, check the description of duties. Will you be working under very close supervision, or will you have responsibility for independent decisions in this work?

4) Choose appropriate study materials

Now that you know the subjects to be examined and the relative amount of each subject to be covered, you can choose suitable study materials. For beginning level jobs, or even advanced ones, if you have a pronounced weakness in some aspect of your training, read a modern, standard textbook in that field. Be sure it is up to date and has general coverage. Such books are normally available at your library, and the librarian will be glad to help you locate one. For entry-level positions, questions of appropriate difficulty are chosen – neither highly advanced questions, nor those too simple. Such questions require careful thought but not advanced training.

If the position for which you are applying is technical or advanced, you will read more advanced, specialized material. If you are already familiar with the basic principles of your field, elementary textbooks would waste your time. Concentrate on advanced textbooks and technical periodicals. Think through the concepts and review difficult problems in your field.

These are all general sources. You can get more ideas on your own initiative, following these leads. For example, training manuals and publications of the government agency which employs workers in your field can be useful, particularly for technical and professional positions. A letter or visit to the government department involved may result in more specific study suggestions, and certainly will provide you with a more definite idea of the exact nature of the position you are seeking.

III. KINDS OF TESTS

Tests are used for purposes other than measuring knowledge and ability to perform specified duties. For some positions, it is equally important to test ability to make adjustments to new situations or to profit from training. In others, basic mental abilities not dependent on information are essential. Questions which test these things may not appear as pertinent to the duties of the position as those which test for knowledge and information. Yet they are often highly important parts of a fair examination. For very general questions, it is almost impossible to help you direct your study efforts. What we can do is to point out some of the more common of these general abilities needed in public service positions and describe some typical questions.

1) General information

Broad, general information has been found useful for predicting job success in some kinds of work. This is tested in a variety of ways, from vocabulary lists to questions about current events. Basic background in some field of work, such as sociology or economics, may be sampled in a group of questions. Often these are principles which have become familiar to most persons through exposure rather than through formal training. It is difficult to advise you how to study for these questions; being alert to the world around you is our best suggestion.

2) Verbal ability

An example of an ability needed in many positions is verbal or language ability. Verbal ability is, in brief, the ability to use and understand words. Vocabulary and grammar tests are typical measures of this ability. Reading comprehension or paragraph interpretation questions are common in many kinds of civil service tests. You are given a paragraph of written material and asked to find its central meaning.

3) Numerical ability

Number skills can be tested by the familiar arithmetic problem, by checking paired lists of numbers to see which are alike and which are different, or by interpreting charts and graphs. In the latter test, a graph may be printed in the test booklet which you are asked to use as the basis for answering questions.

4) Observation

A popular test for law-enforcement positions is the observation test. A picture is shown to you for several minutes, then taken away. Questions about the picture test your ability to observe both details and larger elements.

5) Following directions

In many positions in the public service, the employee must be able to carry out written instructions dependably and accurately. You may be given a chart with several columns, each column listing a variety of information. The questions require you to carry out directions involving the information given in the chart.

6) Skills and aptitudes

Performance tests effectively measure some manual skills and aptitudes. When the skill is one in which you are trained, such as typing or shorthand, you can practice. These tests are often very much like those given in business school or high school courses. For many of the other skills and aptitudes, however, no short-time preparation can be made. Skills and abilities natural to you or that you have developed throughout your lifetime are being tested.

Many of the general questions just described provide all the data needed to answer the questions and ask you to use your reasoning ability to find the answers. Your best preparation for these tests, as well as for tests of facts and ideas, is to be at your physical and mental best. You, no doubt, have your own methods of getting into an exam-taking mood and keeping "in shape." The next section lists some ideas on this subject.

IV. KINDS OF QUESTIONS

Only rarely is the "essay" question, which you answer in narrative form, used in civil service tests. Civil service tests are usually of the short-answer type. Full instructions for answering these questions will be given to you at the examination. But in case this is your first experience with short-answer questions and separate answer sheets, here is what you need to know:

1) Multiple-choice Questions

Most popular of the short-answer questions is the "multiple choice" or "best answer" question. It can be used, for example, to test for factual knowledge, ability to solve problems or judgment in meeting situations found at work.

A multiple-choice question is normally one of three types—
- It can begin with an incomplete statement followed by several possible endings. You are to find the one ending which *best* completes the statement, although some of the others may not be entirely wrong.
- It can also be a complete statement in the form of a question which is answered by choosing one of the statements listed.

- It can be in the form of a problem – again you select the best answer.

Here is an example of a multiple-choice question with a discussion which should give you some clues as to the method for choosing the right answer:

When an employee has a complaint about his assignment, the action which will *best* help him overcome his difficulty is to
   A. discuss his difficulty with his coworkers
   B. take the problem to the head of the organization
   C. take the problem to the person who gave him the assignment
   D. say nothing to anyone about his complaint

In answering this question, you should study each of the choices to find which is best. Consider choice "A" – Certainly an employee may discuss his complaint with fellow employees, but no change or improvement can result, and the complaint remains unresolved. Choice "B" is a poor choice since the head of the organization probably does not know what assignment you have been given, and taking your problem to him is known as "going over the head" of the supervisor. The supervisor, or person who made the assignment, is the person who can clarify it or correct any injustice. Choice "C" is, therefore, correct. To say nothing, as in choice "D," is unwise. Supervisors have and interest in knowing the problems employees are facing, and the employee is seeking a solution to his problem.

2) True/False Questions

The "true/false" or "right/wrong" form of question is sometimes used. Here a complete statement is given. Your job is to decide whether the statement is right or wrong.

SAMPLE: A roaming cell-phone call to a nearby city costs less than a non-roaming call to a distant city.

This statement is wrong, or false, since roaming calls are more expensive.

This is not a complete list of all possible question forms, although most of the others are variations of these common types. You will always get complete directions for answering questions. Be sure you understand *how* to mark your answers – ask questions until you do.

V. RECORDING YOUR ANSWERS

Computer terminals are used more and more today for many different kinds of exams.

For an examination with very few applicants, you may be told to record your answers in the test booklet itself. Separate answer sheets are much more common. If this separate answer sheet is to be scored by machine – and this is often the case – it is highly important that you mark your answers correctly in order to get credit.

An electronic scoring machine is often used in civil service offices because of the speed with which papers can be scored. Machine-scored answer sheets must be marked with a pencil, which will be given to you. This pencil has a high graphite content which responds to the electronic scoring machine. As a matter of fact, stray dots may register as answers, so do not let your pencil rest on the answer sheet while you are pondering the correct answer. Also, if your pencil lead breaks or is otherwise defective, ask for another.

Since the answer sheet will be dropped in a slot in the scoring machine, be careful not to bend the corners or get the paper crumpled.

The answer sheet normally has five vertical columns of numbers, with 30 numbers to a column. These numbers correspond to the question numbers in your test booklet. After each number, going across the page are four or five pairs of dotted lines. These short dotted lines have small letters or numbers above them. The first two pairs may also have a "T" or "F" above the letters. This indicates that the first two pairs only are to be used if the questions are of the true-false type. If the questions are multiple choice, disregard the "T" and "F" and pay attention only to the small letters or numbers.

Answer your questions in the manner of the sample that follows:

32. The largest city in the United States is
     A. Washington, D.C.
     B. New York City
     C. Chicago
     D. Detroit
     E. San Francisco

1) Choose the answer you think is best. (New York City is the largest, so "B" is correct.)
2) Find the row of dotted lines numbered the same as the question you are answering. (Find row number 32)
3) Find the pair of dotted lines corresponding to the answer. (Find the pair of lines under the mark "B.")
4) Make a solid black mark between the dotted lines.

VI. BEFORE THE TEST

Common sense will help you find procedures to follow to get ready for an examination. Too many of us, however, overlook these sensible measures. Indeed, nervousness and fatigue have been found to be the most serious reasons why applicants fail to do their best on civil service tests. Here is a list of reminders:

- Begin your preparation early – Don't wait until the last minute to go scurrying around for books and materials or to find out what the position is all about.
- Prepare continuously – An hour a night for a week is better than an all-night cram session. This has been definitely established. What is more, a night a week for a month will return better dividends than crowding your study into a shorter period of time.
- Locate the place of the exam – You have been sent a notice telling you when and where to report for the examination. If the location is in a different town or otherwise unfamiliar to you, it would be well to inquire the best route and learn something about the building.
- Relax the night before the test – Allow your mind to rest. Do not study at all that night. Plan some mild recreation or diversion; then go to bed early and get a good night's sleep.
- Get up early enough to make a leisurely trip to the place for the test – This way unforeseen events, traffic snarls, unfamiliar buildings, etc. will not upset you.
- Dress comfortably – A written test is not a fashion show. You will be known by number and not by name, so wear something comfortable.

- Leave excess paraphernalia at home – Shopping bags and odd bundles will get in your way. You need bring only the items mentioned in the official notice you received; usually everything you need is provided. Do not bring reference books to the exam. They will only confuse those last minutes and be taken away from you when in the test room.
- Arrive somewhat ahead of time – If because of transportation schedules you must get there very early, bring a newspaper or magazine to take your mind off yourself while waiting.
- Locate the examination room – When you have found the proper room, you will be directed to the seat or part of the room where you will sit. Sometimes you are given a sheet of instructions to read while you are waiting. Do not fill out any forms until you are told to do so; just read them and be prepared.
- Relax and prepare to listen to the instructions
- If you have any physical problem that may keep you from doing your best, be sure to tell the test administrator. If you are sick or in poor health, you really cannot do your best on the exam. You can come back and take the test some other time.

VII. AT THE TEST

The day of the test is here and you have the test booklet in your hand. The temptation to get going is very strong. Caution! There is more to success than knowing the right answers. You must know how to identify your papers and understand variations in the type of short-answer question used in this particular examination. Follow these suggestions for maximum results from your efforts:

1) Cooperate with the monitor
The test administrator has a duty to create a situation in which you can be as much at ease as possible. He will give instructions, tell you when to begin, check to see that you are marking your answer sheet correctly, and so on. He is not there to guard you, although he will see that your competitors do not take unfair advantage. He wants to help you do your best.

2) Listen to all instructions
Don't jump the gun! Wait until you understand all directions. In most civil service tests you get more time than you need to answer the questions. So don't be in a hurry. Read each word of instructions until you clearly understand the meaning. Study the examples, listen to all announcements and follow directions. Ask questions if you do not understand what to do.

3) Identify your papers
Civil service exams are usually identified by number only. You will be assigned a number; you must not put your name on your test papers. Be sure to copy your number correctly. Since more than one exam may be given, copy your exact examination title.

4) Plan your time
Unless you are told that a test is a "speed" or "rate of work" test, speed itself is usually not important. Time enough to answer all the questions will be provided, but this does not mean that you have all day. An overall time limit has been set. Divide the total time (in minutes) by the number of questions to determine the approximate time you have for each question.

5) Do not linger over difficult questions

If you come across a difficult question, mark it with a paper clip (useful to have along) and come back to it when you have been through the booklet. One caution if you do this – be sure to skip a number on your answer sheet as well. Check often to be sure that you have not lost your place and that you are marking in the row numbered the same as the question you are answering.

6) Read the questions

Be sure you know what the question asks! Many capable people are unsuccessful because they failed to *read* the questions correctly.

7) Answer all questions

Unless you have been instructed that a penalty will be deducted for incorrect answers, it is better to guess than to omit a question.

8) Speed tests

It is often better NOT to guess on speed tests. It has been found that on timed tests people are tempted to spend the last few seconds before time is called in marking answers at random – without even reading them – in the hope of picking up a few extra points. To discourage this practice, the instructions may warn you that your score will be "corrected" for guessing. That is, a penalty will be applied. The incorrect answers will be deducted from the correct ones, or some other penalty formula will be used.

9) Review your answers

If you finish before time is called, go back to the questions you guessed or omitted to give them further thought. Review other answers if you have time.

10) Return your test materials

If you are ready to leave before others have finished or time is called, take ALL your materials to the monitor and leave quietly. Never take any test material with you. The monitor can discover whose papers are not complete, and taking a test booklet may be grounds for disqualification.

VIII. EXAMINATION TECHNIQUES

1) Read the general instructions carefully. These are usually printed on the first page of the exam booklet. As a rule, these instructions refer to the timing of the examination; the fact that you should not start work until the signal and must stop work at a signal, etc. If there are any *special* instructions, such as a choice of questions to be answered, make sure that you note this instruction carefully.

2) When you are ready to start work on the examination, that is as soon as the signal has been given, read the instructions to each question booklet, underline any key words or phrases, such as *least, best, outline, describe* and the like. In this way you will tend to answer as requested rather than discover on reviewing your paper that you *listed without describing*, that you selected the *worst* choice rather than the *best* choice, etc.

3) If the examination is of the objective or multiple-choice type – that is, each question will also give a series of possible answers: A, B, C or D, and you are called upon to select the best answer and write the letter next to that answer on your answer paper – it is advisable to start answering each question in turn. There may be anywhere from 50 to 100 such questions in the three or four hours allotted and you can see how much time would be taken if you read through all the questions before beginning to answer any. Furthermore, if you come across a question or group of questions which you know would be difficult to answer, it would undoubtedly affect your handling of all the other questions.

4) If the examination is of the essay type and contains but a few questions, it is a moot point as to whether you should read all the questions before starting to answer any one. Of course, if you are given a choice – say five out of seven and the like – then it is essential to read all the questions so you can eliminate the two that are most difficult. If, however, you are asked to answer all the questions, there may be danger in trying to answer the easiest one first because you may find that you will spend too much time on it. The best technique is to answer the first question, then proceed to the second, etc.

5) Time your answers. Before the exam begins, write down the time it started, then add the time allowed for the examination and write down the time it must be completed, then divide the time available somewhat as follows:
   - If 3-1/2 hours are allowed, that would be 210 minutes. If you have 80 objective-type questions, that would be an average of 2-1/2 minutes per question. Allow yourself no more than 2 minutes per question, or a total of 160 minutes, which will permit about 50 minutes to review.
   - If for the time allotment of 210 minutes there are 7 essay questions to answer, that would average about 30 minutes a question. Give yourself only 25 minutes per question so that you have about 35 minutes to review.

6) The most important instruction is to *read each question* and make sure you know what is wanted. The second most important instruction is to *time yourself properly* so that you answer every question. The third most important instruction is to *answer every question.* Guess if you have to but include something for each question. Remember that you will receive no credit for a blank and will probably receive some credit if you write something in answer to an essay question. If you guess a letter – say "B" for a multiple-choice question – you may have guessed right. If you leave a blank as an answer to a multiple-choice question, the examiners may respect your feelings but it will not add a point to your score. Some exams may penalize you for wrong answers, so in such cases *only*, you may not want to guess unless you have some basis for your answer.

7) Suggestions
   a. Objective-type questions
      1. Examine the question booklet for proper sequence of pages and questions
      2. Read all instructions carefully
      3. Skip any question which seems too difficult; return to it after all other questions have been answered
      4. Apportion your time properly; do not spend too much time on any single question or group of questions

5. Note and underline key words – *all, most, fewest, least, best, worst, same, opposite,* etc.
6. Pay particular attention to negatives
7. Note unusual option, e.g., unduly long, short, complex, different or similar in content to the body of the question
8. Observe the use of "hedging" words – *probably, may, most likely,* etc.
9. Make sure that your answer is put next to the same number as the question
10. Do not second-guess unless you have good reason to believe the second answer is definitely more correct
11. Cross out original answer if you decide another answer is more accurate; do not erase until you are ready to hand your paper in
12. Answer all questions; guess unless instructed otherwise
13. Leave time for review

   b. Essay questions
1. Read each question carefully
2. Determine exactly what is wanted. Underline key words or phrases.
3. Decide on outline or paragraph answer
4. Include many different points and elements unless asked to develop any one or two points or elements
5. Show impartiality by giving pros and cons unless directed to select one side only
6. Make and write down any assumptions you find necessary to answer the questions
7. Watch your English, grammar, punctuation and choice of words
8. Time your answers; don't crowd material

8) Answering the essay question

Most essay questions can be answered by framing the specific response around several key words or ideas. Here are a few such key words or ideas:

M's: manpower, materials, methods, money, management
P's: purpose, program, policy, plan, procedure, practice, problems, pitfalls, personnel, public relations
   a. Six basic steps in handling problems:
1. Preliminary plan and background development
2. Collect information, data and facts
3. Analyze and interpret information, data and facts
4. Analyze and develop solutions as well as make recommendations
5. Prepare report and sell recommendations
6. Install recommendations and follow up effectiveness

   b. Pitfalls to avoid
1. *Taking things for granted* – A statement of the situation does not necessarily imply that each of the elements is necessarily true; for example, a complaint may be invalid and biased so that all that can be taken for granted is that a complaint has been registered

2. *Considering only one side of a situation* – Wherever possible, indicate several alternatives and then point out the reasons you selected the best one
3. *Failing to indicate follow up* – Whenever your answer indicates action on your part, make certain that you will take proper follow-up action to see how successful your recommendations, procedures or actions turn out to be
4. *Taking too long in answering any single question* – Remember to time your answers properly

IX. AFTER THE TEST

Scoring procedures differ in detail among civil service jurisdictions although the general principles are the same. Whether the papers are hand-scored or graded by machine we have described, they are nearly always graded by number. That is, the person who marks the paper knows only the number – never the name – of the applicant. Not until all the papers have been graded will they be matched with names. If other tests, such as training and experience or oral interview ratings have been given, scores will be combined. Different parts of the examination usually have different weights. For example, the written test might count 60 percent of the final grade, and a rating of training and experience 40 percent. In many jurisdictions, veterans will have a certain number of points added to their grades.

After the final grade has been determined, the names are placed in grade order and an eligible list is established. There are various methods for resolving ties between those who get the same final grade – probably the most common is to place first the name of the person whose application was received first. Job offers are made from the eligible list in the order the names appear on it. You will be notified of your grade and your rank as soon as all these computations have been made. This will be done as rapidly as possible.

People who are found to meet the requirements in the announcement are called "eligibles." Their names are put on a list of eligible candidates. An eligible's chances of getting a job depend on how high he stands on this list and how fast agencies are filling jobs from the list.

When a job is to be filled from a list of eligibles, the agency asks for the names of people on the list of eligibles for that job. When the civil service commission receives this request, it sends to the agency the names of the three people highest on this list. Or, if the job to be filled has specialized requirements, the office sends the agency the names of the top three persons who meet these requirements from the general list.

The appointing officer makes a choice from among the three people whose names were sent to him. If the selected person accepts the appointment, the names of the others are put back on the list to be considered for future openings.

That is the rule in hiring from all kinds of eligible lists, whether they are for typist, carpenter, chemist, or something else. For every vacancy, the appointing officer has his choice of any one of the top three eligibles on the list. This explains why the person whose name is on top of the list sometimes does not get an appointment when some of the persons lower on the list do. If the appointing officer chooses the second or third eligible, the No. 1 eligible does not get a job at once, but stays on the list until he is appointed or the list is terminated.

X. HOW TO PASS THE INTERVIEW TEST

The examination for which you applied requires an oral interview test. You have already taken the written test and you are now being called for the interview test – the final part of the formal examination.

You may think that it is not possible to prepare for an interview test and that there are no procedures to follow during an interview. Our purpose is to point out some things you can do in advance that will help you and some good rules to follow and pitfalls to avoid while you are being interviewed.

What is an interview supposed to test?

The written examination is designed to test the technical knowledge and competence of the candidate; the oral is designed to evaluate intangible qualities, not readily measured otherwise, and to establish a list showing the relative fitness of each candidate – as measured against his competitors – for the position sought. Scoring is not on the basis of "right" and "wrong," but on a sliding scale of values ranging from "not passable" to "outstanding." As a matter of fact, it is possible to achieve a relatively low score without a single "incorrect" answer because of evident weakness in the qualities being measured.

Occasionally, an examination may consist entirely of an oral test – either an individual or a group oral. In such cases, information is sought concerning the technical knowledges and abilities of the candidate, since there has been no written examination for this purpose. More commonly, however, an oral test is used to supplement a written examination.

Who conducts interviews?

The composition of oral boards varies among different jurisdictions. In nearly all, a representative of the personnel department serves as chairman. One of the members of the board may be a representative of the department in which the candidate would work. In some cases, "outside experts" are used, and, frequently, a businessman or some other representative of the general public is asked to serve. Labor and management or other special groups may be represented. The aim is to secure the services of experts in the appropriate field.

However the board is composed, it is a good idea (and not at all improper or unethical) to ascertain in advance of the interview who the members are and what groups they represent. When you are introduced to them, you will have some idea of their backgrounds and interests, and at least you will not stutter and stammer over their names.

What should be done before the interview?

While knowledge about the board members is useful and takes some of the surprise element out of the interview, there is other preparation which is more substantive. It *is* possible to prepare for an oral interview – in several ways:

1) Keep a copy of your application and review it carefully before the interview

This may be the only document before the oral board, and the starting point of the interview. Know what education and experience you have listed there, and the sequence and dates of all of it. Sometimes the board will ask you to review the highlights of your experience for them; you should not have to hem and haw doing it.

2) Study the class specification and the examination announcement

Usually, the oral board has one or both of these to guide them. The qualities, characteristics or knowledges required by the position sought are stated in these documents. They offer valuable clues as to the nature of the oral interview. For example, if the job involves supervisory responsibilities, the announcement will usually indicate that knowledge of modern supervisory methods and the qualifications of the candidate as a supervisor will be tested. If so, you can expect such questions, frequently in the form of a hypothetical situation which you are expected to solve. NEVER go into an oral without knowledge of the duties and responsibilities of the job you seek.

3) Think through each qualification required

Try to visualize the kind of questions you would ask if you were a board member. How well could you answer them? Try especially to appraise your own knowledge and background in each area, *measured against the job sought*, and identify any areas in which you are weak. Be critical and realistic – do not flatter yourself.

4) Do some general reading in areas in which you feel you may be weak

For example, if the job involves supervision and your past experience has NOT, some general reading in supervisory methods and practices, particularly in the field of human relations, might be useful. Do NOT study agency procedures or detailed manuals. The oral board will be testing your understanding and capacity, not your memory.

5) Get a good night's sleep and watch your general health and mental attitude

You will want a clear head at the interview. Take care of a cold or any other minor ailment, and of course, no hangovers.

What should be done on the day of the interview?

Now comes the day of the interview itself. Give yourself plenty of time to get there. Plan to arrive somewhat ahead of the scheduled time, particularly if your appointment is in the fore part of the day. If a previous candidate fails to appear, the board might be ready for you a bit early. By early afternoon an oral board is almost invariably behind schedule if there are many candidates, and you may have to wait. Take along a book or magazine to read, or your application to review, but leave any extraneous material in the waiting room when you go in for your interview. In any event, relax and compose yourself.

The matter of dress is important. The board is forming impressions about you – from your experience, your manners, your attitude, and your appearance. Give your personal appearance careful attention. Dress your best, but not your flashiest. Choose conservative, appropriate clothing, and be sure it is immaculate. This is a business interview, and your appearance should indicate that you regard it as such. Besides, being well groomed and properly dressed will help boost your confidence.

Sooner or later, someone will call your name and escort you into the interview room. *This is it.* From here on you are on your own. It is too late for any more preparation. But remember, you asked for this opportunity to prove your fitness, and you are here because your request was granted.

What happens when you go in?

The usual sequence of events will be as follows: The clerk (who is often the board stenographer) will introduce you to the chairman of the oral board, who will introduce you to the other members of the board. Acknowledge the introductions before you sit down. Do not be surprised if you find a microphone facing you or a stenotypist sitting by. Oral interviews are usually recorded in the event of an appeal or other review.

Usually the chairman of the board will open the interview by reviewing the highlights of your education and work experience from your application – primarily for the benefit of the other members of the board, as well as to get the material into the record. Do not interrupt or comment unless there is an error or significant misinterpretation; if that is the case, do not hesitate. But do not quibble about insignificant matters. Also, he will usually ask you some question about your education, experience or your present job – partly to get you to start talking and to establish the interviewing "rapport." He may start the actual questioning, or turn it over to one of the other members. Frequently, each member undertakes the questioning on a particular area, one in which he is perhaps most competent, so you can expect each member to participate in the examination. Because time is limited, you may also expect some rather abrupt switches in the direction the questioning takes, so do not be upset by it. Normally, a board member will not pursue a single line of questioning unless he discovers a particular strength or weakness.

After each member has participated, the chairman will usually ask whether any member has any further questions, then will ask you if you have anything you wish to add. Unless you are expecting this question, it may floor you. Worse, it may start you off on an extended, extemporaneous speech. The board is not usually seeking more information. The question is principally to offer you a last opportunity to present further qualifications or to indicate that you have nothing to add. So, if you feel that a significant qualification or characteristic has been overlooked, it is proper to point it out in a sentence or so. Do not compliment the board on the thoroughness of their examination – they have been sketchy, and you know it. If you wish, merely say, "No thank you, I have nothing further to add." This is a point where you can "talk yourself out" of a good impression or fail to present an important bit of information. Remember, *you close the interview yourself.*

The chairman will then say, "That is all, Mr. _____, thank you." Do not be startled; the interview is over, and quicker than you think. Thank him, gather your belongings and take your leave. Save your sigh of relief for the other side of the door.

How to put your best foot forward

Throughout this entire process, you may feel that the board individually and collectively is trying to pierce your defenses, seek out your hidden weaknesses and embarrass and confuse you. Actually, this is not true. They are obliged to make an appraisal of your qualifications for the job you are seeking, and they want to see you in your best light. Remember, they must interview all candidates and a non-cooperative candidate may become a failure in spite of their best efforts to bring out his qualifications. Here are 15 suggestions that will help you:

1) Be natural – Keep your attitude confident, not cocky

If you are not confident that you can do the job, do not expect the board to be. Do not apologize for your weaknesses, try to bring out your strong points. The board is interested in a positive, not negative, presentation. Cockiness will antagonize any board member and make him wonder if you are covering up a weakness by a false show of strength.

2) Get comfortable, but don't lounge or sprawl

Sit erectly but not stiffly. A careless posture may lead the board to conclude that you are careless in other things, or at least that you are not impressed by the importance of the occasion. Either conclusion is natural, even if incorrect. Do not fuss with your clothing, a pencil or an ashtray. Your hands may occasionally be useful to emphasize a point; do not let them become a point of distraction.

3) Do not wisecrack or make small talk

This is a serious situation, and your attitude should show that you consider it as such. Further, the time of the board is limited – they do not want to waste it, and neither should you.

4) Do not exaggerate your experience or abilities

In the first place, from information in the application or other interviews and sources, the board may know more about you than you think. Secondly, you probably will not get away with it. An experienced board is rather adept at spotting such a situation, so do not take the chance.

5) If you know a board member, do not make a point of it, yet do not hide it

Certainly you are not fooling him, and probably not the other members of the board. Do not try to take advantage of your acquaintanceship – it will probably do you little good.

6) Do not dominate the interview

Let the board do that. They will give you the clues – do not assume that you have to do all the talking. Realize that the board has a number of questions to ask you, and do not try to take up all the interview time by showing off your extensive knowledge of the answer to the first one.

7) Be attentive

You only have 20 minutes or so, and you should keep your attention at its sharpest throughout. When a member is addressing a problem or question to you, give him your undivided attention. Address your reply principally to him, but do not exclude the other board members.

8) Do not interrupt

A board member may be stating a problem for you to analyze. He will ask you a question when the time comes. Let him state the problem, and wait for the question.

9) Make sure you understand the question

Do not try to answer until you are sure what the question is. If it is not clear, restate it in your own words or ask the board member to clarify it for you. However, do not haggle about minor elements.

10) Reply promptly but not hastily

A common entry on oral board rating sheets is "candidate responded readily," or "candidate hesitated in replies." Respond as promptly and quickly as you can, but do not jump to a hasty, ill-considered answer.

11) Do not be peremptory in your answers

A brief answer is proper – but do not fire your answer back. That is a losing game from your point of view. The board member can probably ask questions much faster than you can answer them.

12) Do not try to create the answer you think the board member wants

He is interested in what kind of mind you have and how it works – not in playing games. Furthermore, he can usually spot this practice and will actually grade you down on it.

13) Do not switch sides in your reply merely to agree with a board member

Frequently, a member will take a contrary position merely to draw you out and to see if you are willing and able to defend your point of view. Do not start a debate, yet do not surrender a good position. If a position is worth taking, it is worth defending.

14) Do not be afraid to admit an error in judgment if you are shown to be wrong

The board knows that you are forced to reply without any opportunity for careful consideration. Your answer may be demonstrably wrong. If so, admit it and get on with the interview.

15) Do not dwell at length on your present job

The opening question may relate to your present assignment. Answer the question but do not go into an extended discussion. You are being examined for a *new* job, not your present one. As a matter of fact, try to phrase ALL your answers in terms of the job for which you are being examined.

Basis of Rating

Probably you will forget most of these "do's" and "don'ts" when you walk into the oral interview room. Even remembering them all will not ensure you a passing grade. Perhaps you did not have the qualifications in the first place. But remembering them will help you to put your best foot forward, without treading on the toes of the board members.

Rumor and popular opinion to the contrary notwithstanding, an oral board wants you to make the best appearance possible. They know you are under pressure – but they also want to see how you respond to it as a guide to what your reaction would be under the pressures of the job you seek. They will be influenced by the degree of poise you display, the personal traits you show and the manner in which you respond.

ABOUT THIS BOOK

This book contains tests divided into Examination Sections. Go through each test, answering every question in the margin. We have also attached a sample answer sheet at the back of the book that can be removed and used. At the end of each test look at the answer key and check your answers. On the ones you got wrong, look at the right answer choice and learn. Do not fill in the answers first. Do not memorize the questions and answers, but understand the answer and principles involved. On your test, the questions will likely be different from the samples. Questions are changed and new ones added. If you understand these past questions you should have success with any changes that arise. Tests may consist of several types of questions. We have additional books on each subject should more study be advisable or necessary for you. Finally, the more you study, the better prepared you will be. This book is intended to be the last thing you study before you walk into the examination room. Prior study of relevant texts is also recommended. NLC publishes some of these in our Fundamental Series. Knowledge and good sense are important factors in passing your exam. Good luck also helps. So now study this Passbook, absorb the material contained within and take that knowledge into the examination. Then do your best to pass that exam.

EXAMINATION SECTION

EXAMINATION SECTION
TEST 1

DIRECTIONS: Each question or incomplete statement is followed by several suggested answers or completions. Select the one that BEST answers the question or completes the statement. *PRINT THE LETTER OF THE CORRECT ANSWER IN THE SPACE AT THE RIGHT.*

1. An effective method to correct mirror writing by the intellectually disabled is to   1._____

    A. have him write looking through a mirror
    B. have him change from use of left hand to the right hand
    C. re-emphasize the correct posture and position for writing
    D. have him copy models showing the starting point of writing

2. Dr. Robert Guthrie developed a blood test to be administered to infants to detect the presence of   2._____

    A. syphilis
    C. hydrocephalus
    B. hypothyroidism
    D. phenylketonuria

3. Which of the following defines intellectual disability as a disability characterized by significant limitations both in intellectual functioning and in adaptive behavior, originating before age 18 and covering a range of everyday social and practical skills?   3._____

    A. American Association on Intellectual and Developmental Disabilities
    B. E.A. Doll
    C. Council for Exceptional Children
    D. Clemens Benda

4. Early studies on the nature of intelligence revealed that the BEST predictors of intelligence for school-age children were _____ tasks.   4._____

    A. simple sensori-motor
    C. speed of reaction to timed
    B. complex sensori-motor
    D. complex verbal

5. Which of the following conditions automatically warrants the exclusion of intellectually disabled children from school attendance?   5._____

    A. Lack of toilet training
    C. Aphasia
    B. Petit-mal epilepsy
    D. Anxiety

6. Which one of the following state agencies is assigned the responsibility for carrying out planning in intellectual disablities? Department of   6._____

    A. Education
    C. Labor
    B. Welfare
    D. Mental Hygiene

7. Which one of the following publications dealt exclusively with intellectual disablity and related problems?   7._____

    A. THE VOLTA REVIEW
    B. THE TRAINING SCHOOL BULLETIN
    C. EXCEPTIONAL CHILDREN
    D. THE JOURNAL OF GENETIC PSYCHOLOGY

8. *It is just as important to integrate the mentally retarded within our society and make full use of their abilities as it is to make a special effort to do this for the physically handicapped.*
This statement was made by

    A. John F. Kennedy   B. Lyndon B. Johnson
    C. Hubert Humphrey   D. Dwight D. Eisenhower

8.____

9. The study of mental deficiency as a specialized branch of medicine did NOT develop until

    A. Itard demonstrated his success with the Wild Boy of Aveyron
    B. investigators realized that mental defect required treatment dissimilar to that of mental illness
    C. Goddard's work on the inheritance of mental defect was published
    D. Pinel removed the shackles from the patients at the Hospice des Bicetre

9.____

10. The *patterning* method of treating neurologically handicapped children was originated at the Institute

    A. of Neurological Diseases
    B. for the Achievement of Human Potential
    C. of Defectology
    D. for the Crippled and Disabled

10.____

11. Which one of the following may properly be considered the MOST significant recent development in rehabilitation of the intellectually disabled? The

    A. use of new diagnostic techniques with disabled young adults
    B. development of combined school-work programs
    C. use of rehabilitation counselors in the schools
    D. identification of social problems of the intellectually disabled

11.____

12. Which one of the following needs of the intellectually disabled is often minimized?

    A. Diagnosis
    B. Institutionalization
    C. Development of worthwhile leisure time activities
    D. Specially trained teachers

12.____

13. Which of the following is the MOST likely underlying cause of most vandalism in intellectually disabled school-age children?

    A. Compensation for feelings of helplessness
    B. Inadequate protection of property
    C. Delinquent or pre-delinquent personality structure
    D. Intra-gang competitiveness

13.____

14. Of the following, the developer of the *talking typewriter* used with disabled children was

    A. Samuel A. Kirk   B. Albert J. Harris
    C. Paul A. Witty   D. Omar K. Moore

14.____

15. The leaders in the national campaign to treat intellectual disablity recommend that the   15.____
major responsibility for development of programs should be assumed by

    A. the federal government   B. community agencies
    C. state governments   D. municipal governments

16. A recent development in post-school vocational placement of the intellectually disabled is   16.____
the assignment of the responsibility for placement to

    A. guidance counselors of the Board of Education's special education department
    B. community offices of the State Employment Service
    C. selective placement counselors of the Division of Vocational Rehabilitation
    D. special committees functioning within the parent organizations for the disabled

17. Which one of the following is a suitable industrial job operation for which a disabled   17.____
high school student may be trained?

    A. Wire preparation and soldering
    B. Hot water boiler assembly
    C. Steamfitting
    D. Repair work on electric and gas driven lawnmowers

18. The PRIME objective of an educational program for the intellectually disabled   18.____
should be the development of

    A. avocational pursuits and hobbies to fill their leisure time
    B. manipulative ability that will lead to some marketable skills
    C. reading skills that include the basic words in *reading for protection*
    D. general communication skills in both the school and the home

19. In a program of occupational education for the intellectually disabled, vocational guidance   19.____
is interpreted as encompassing

    A. a study of appropriate jobs
    B. help for those with limited vocational potential to find jobs
    C. self-evaluation of individual qualifications against specific job requirements
    D. job placement

20. The average lifespan of an individual with Down syndrome is closest to   20.____

    A. 25   B. 35   C. 50   D. 60

KEY (CORRECT ANSWERS)

1.	D	11.	B
2.	D	12.	C
3.	A	13.	A
4.	D	14.	D
5.	A	15.	C
6.	D	16.	B
7.	B	17.	A
8.	A	18.	D
9.	B	19.	C
10.	B	20.	D

———

TEST 2

DIRECTIONS: Each question or incomplete statement is followed by several suggested answers or completions. Select the one that BEST answers the question or completes the statement. *PRINT THE LETTER OF THE CORRECT ANSWER IN THE SPACE AT THE RIGHT.*

1. In this state, the period of compulsory school attendance for intellectually disabled children is   1._____

    A. the same as that for non-disabled children
    B. shorter than that for non-disabled children
    C. longer than that for non-disabled children
    D. either shorter or longer than that for non-disabled children, depending on the child's actual class progress

2. Recent publications from the federal government estimate the number of intellectually disabled people in the country to be APPROXIMATELY _____ million.   2._____

    A. 2.5   B. 6.5   C. 8.5   D. 11.5

3. A MOST significant legislative event relative to intellectual disablity was the passage of a law   3._____

    A. making it mandatory that all infants be tested for phenylketonuria
    B. subsidizing sheltered workshops on a per capita basis
    C. making it mandatory that emotionally disturbed children be provided with educational programs
    D. providing a salary differential for teachers of handicapped children

4. Which one of the following individuals exerted the GREATEST influence in the training of disabled children?   4._____

    A. Piaget   B. Montessori   C. Freud   D. Seguin

5. The incidence of intellectual disablity is   5._____

    A. greater among males than females
    B. greater among the offspring of the poor than the rich
    C. proportionally greater among Black than among white families
    D. greater among the offspring of uneducated than among offspring of educated families

6. The qualifying conditions for intellectual disablity for different age groups include social adjustment, learning ability, and rate of maturation.   6._____
   Rate of maturation as a factor in intellectual disablity has special significance during the

    A. first few years of life   B. primary school years
    C. adolescent period   D. young adult period

7. Rubella may cause intellectual disablity when contracted by a pregnant woman, particularly during the   7._____

    A. first three months of pregnancy
    B. second three months of pregnancy
    C. third three months of pregnancy
    D. latter half of the pregnancy period

8. Studies of the relative abilities of disabled and normal individuals in learning indicate that the intellectually disabled

    A. show no difference in the rate or amount of learning compared to their normal peers of the same mental age
    B. are less capable in abstracting and generalizing from their experiences
    C. are not affected by the complexity of the task presented
    D. cannot be trained to use verbal cues in learning

9. Which one of the following phases of the Occupational Education program is NOT the responsibility of the teacher?

    A. Occupational information
    B. Vocational guidance
    C. Job placement
    D. Vocational training

10. A program of Occupational Education for the disabled adolescent places GREATEST emphasis upon the development of

    A. personal-social
    B. social-occupational
    C. occupational-academic
    D. academic-personal

11. In a program of Occupational Education for the intellectually disabled, vocational training should emphasize MOST heavily training in

    A. non-manual skills necessary in the work area
    B. general habits, attitudes, and skills common to good workmanship and citizenship
    C. manual skills needed in the work area
    D. measuring individual abilities against job requirements

12. In general, the HIGHEST job level at which an intellectually disabled individual can function in open competitive industry is as a(n)

    A. sheltered helper
    B. skilled worker
    C. semi-skilled worker
    D. unskilled worker

13. Which one of the following is the PRIMARY objective of the Work-Study program for intellectually disabled youth?

    A. Developing a realistic attitude toward school
    B. Determining the types of jobs they will be qualified to hold
    C. Emphasizing proper job attitudes
    D. Helping pupils make a successful transition from school to full-time employment

14. MOST maladoptive behavior of the intellectually disabled child is a function of his

    A. disablity
    B. interpersonal relationships
    C. academic frustrations
    D. faulty perception of the environment

15. The emotional problems exhibited by intellectually disabled children are essentially

    A. the same kind as those exhibited by non-disabled children
    B. dependent primarily upon the clinical classification of disablity
    C. determined by the child's constitutional endowment
    D. qualitatively different from those of children who are not disabled

16. The BEST single diagnostic index of disablity in a young pre-school child with normal visual and auditory capacities is
    16.____

    A. an underdeveloped comprehension and speaking vocabulary for his age
    B. delayed motor development for his age
    C. inability to distinguish stimuli simultaneously presented to the face and hand
    D. an abnormal EEG record

17. According to Stanford-Binet, an IQ between 55 and 69 is _____ impaired or delayed.
    17.____

    A. severely   B. moderately   C. mildly   D. average

18. Down syndrome is associated with
    18.____

    A. head trauma   B. chromosomes   C. nutrition   D. infection

19. Which one of the following is MOST likely to be symptomatic of the defense mechanism known as *regression* in an older disabled child?
    19.____

    A. Sudden immature behavior in a class
    B. Constant *forgetting* to do a class assignment
    C. Affirming that a dead parent is still alive
    D. Acting like another well-liked child in the class

20. To which one of the following therapeutic techniques is the use of role playing as a guidance tool MOST closely related?
    20.____

    A. Group therapy   B. Free association
    C. Psychotherapy   D. Psychodrama

KEY (CORRECT ANSWERS)

1.	A		11.	B
2.	B		12.	C
3.	A		13.	D
4.	D		14.	B
5.	A		15.	A
6.	A		16.	A
7.	A		17.	C
8.	B		18.	B
9.	C		19.	A
10.	B		20.	D

———

EXAMINATION SECTION
TEST 1

DIRECTIONS: Each question or incomplete statement is followed by several suggested answers or completions. Select the one that BEST answers the question or completes the statement. *PRINT THE LETTER OF THE CORRECT ANSWER IN THE SPACE AT THE RIGHT.*

1. Clinical observations and research on motor functioning of the intellectually disabled indicate   1.____

    A. there is a marked discrepancy in motor functioning between tasks requiring precise and those requiring complex movements
    B. there is a high degree of correspondence between general mental ability and motor performance
    C. there is no difference in the motor performance of moderately disabled and mildly disabled individuals
    D. degree of stimulation has no effect on motor performance

2. The incidence of the diagnosis of intellectual disability in males as compared with that of females is   2.____

    A. considerably higher   B. considerably lower
    C. slightly lower   D. about the same

3. In terms of their behavior and the causes of their disability, intellectually disabled children would be classified as a _____ group.   3.____

    A. very homogeneous   B. moderately homogeneous
    C. very heterogeneous   D. moderately heterogeneous

4. In terms of socioeconomic status, MOST disabled children come from families that in socioeconomic status   4.____

    A. are rated low
    B. range from middle class to high
    C. are middle class
    D. range the spectrum

5. While phenylketonuria accounts for a small fraction of intellectual disabilities, it is one of the few forms that can be   5.____

    A. identified as a causative agent in the first three months of pregnancy
    B. vitiated by early psychiatric treatment
    C. alleviated through strict adherence to a high phenyla-lanine diet
    D. prevented by specific medical intervention

6. A child who has been diagnosed as having cerebral aphasia shows _____ speech.   6.____

    A. lack of   B. perseverative   C. echolalic   D. repetitive

7. Follow-up studies indicate that the intellectually disabled tend to   7.____

    A. remain on their initial job because they are fearful of change
    B. change jobs frequently in their early post-school years
    C. move up the ladder of success as do non-disabled, but at a slower pace
    D. stabilize in one job or one area of work in their early post-school years

8. The PRIMARY objective of special education for the preponderance of the intellectually disabled is

    A. contribution to the community
    B. participation in family life
    C. adjustment to the neighborhood environment
    D. adjustment in a sheltered work situation

9. Disability resulting from organic impairment or birth injury has been classified as

    A. endogenous
    C. primary amentia
    B. familial
    D. exogenous

10. Resources in the community for treating the emotional problems of intellectually disabled children are

    A. more difficult to obtain than for non-disabled children
    B. under-utilized because of parental resistance to accepting disabilities
    C. under-utilized because the disabilities tend to mask emotional difficulties
    D. not effective with most types of disabled children

11. The disabled child who refuses to attend school and cries, throws up, and clings to the parent when it comes time to leave each morning is MOST probably showing symptoms of

    A. overdependence
    C. psychopathic behavior
    B. school phobia
    D. improper nutrition

12. One of the MOST promising developments in institutional care for the intellectually disabled was the

    A. addition of attendants to the inter-disciplinary staffs of installations
    B. organization of a well-rounded recreation program
    C. inclusion of psychotherapy in the institutional program
    D. establishment of a self-government program

13. The Arc is a(n)

    A. youth group for the disabled, similar in design to the 4-H Clubs
    B. group of non-professionals associated with the American Association on Mental Deficiency
    C. service and support organization for disabled individuals and their families
    D. association of teachers of the disabled, organized by the National Education Association

14. In MOST instances, parental inability to accept disabilities in their child as a fact can be attributed primarily to their

    A. feelings of guilt
    B. fear of being viewed as subnormal themselves
    C. lack of knowledge of children's development
    D. being too close to the child to see him objectively

15. Which one of the following descriptions MOST accurately characterizes the degree to   15.____
which the intellectually disabled will be able to function in social-vocational areas when
they reach adulthood?

    A. Little more than self-care
    B. Partial self-support in a supervised environment, such as a sheltered workshop
    C. Employment, when given assistance from medical personnel in correcting physical
       or emotional deficiencies
    D. Employment in the community with the aid of appropriate school and community
       agencies when necessary

16. The process whereby an individual acquires his moral, social, and emotional attitudes   16.____
from the people with whom he comes in frequent contact is called

    A. projection   B. introjection
    C. transfer of learning   D. transference

17. A resident of working age, who has a permanent disability that is an employment   17.____
handicap, is eligible for vocational rehabilitation if he

    A. is unemployable
    B. requires custodial care for an extended period of time
    C. is employable in a sheltered workshop only
    D. can become employable within a reasonable length of time

18. Of those listed below, the MOST likely jobs for the intellectually disabled are: 18.____

    A. Messenger, hospital tray worker
    B. Foot press operator, practical nurse
    C. Shoeshine man, barber
    D. Plumber's helper, elevator operator

19. Of the following, which one is the MOST common etiological factor in clinical cases of   19.____
intellectual disability?

    A. Phenylketonuria   B. Down syndrome
    C. Organic brain damage   D. Environmental deprivation

20. Which of the following types of recreational activity are MOST appropriate for the   20.____
intellectually disabled?

    A. Basketball, swimming   B. Dancing, bowling
    C. Football, boxing   D. Stickball, roller skating

KEY (CORRECT ANSWERS)

1.	B	11.	B
2.	A	12.	D
3.	C	13.	C
4.	D	14.	A
5.	D	15.	D
6.	A	16.	B
7.	B	17.	D
8.	A	18.	A
9.	D	19.	C
10.	A	20.	B

———

TEST 2

DIRECTIONS: Each question or incomplete statement is followed by several suggested answers or completions. Select the one that BEST answers the question or completes the statement. *PRINT THE LETTER OF THE CORRECT ANSWER IN THE SPACE AT THE RIGHT.*

1. The instructional program for the intellectually disabled stresses   1.____

   A. association   B. configuration
   C. perseveration   D. habit formation

2. Of the following, the MAJOR goal of the education of disabled children is to enable them to   2.____

   A. become skilled workers in selected jobs
   B. develop a better understanding of their problems and make a better adjustment to them
   C. become completely socially adequate in their communities
   D. develop qualities of leadership in limited areas

3. The MAJOR way in which the development of the disabled child resembles that of the   3.____
   normal child in the early years of life is in the attainment of

   A. locomotion skills   B. manual dexterity
   C. language skills   D. physical size

4. The terminology used in characterizing the disabled has changed over the years.   4.____
   Which one of the following CORRECTLY gives the order in which past terms have appeared?

   A. Mentally deficient, mentally handicapped, feebleminded
   B. Mentally deficient, feebleminded, mentally retarded
   C. Feebleminded, mentally deficient, mentally retarded
   D. Mentally retarded, feebleminded, mentally deficient

5. As the severely disabled child approaches adolescence and adulthood, there is a ten-   5.____
   dency for the IQ to

   A. decline
   B. remain static
   C. show slight but positive increases
   D. show significant increases

6. When used with reference to intellectually disabled children, the term *adaptive behavior*   6.____
   refers to the child's

   A. ability to shift readily from one learning situation to another
   B. prognosis for anti-social behavior
   C. effectiveness in coping with the social demands of the environment
   D. functioning level as determined by a projective testing technique

7. In presenting areas of interest for the disabled adolescent: 7.____
      I.   Budgeting
      II. Study of Job Areas
      III. The Worker as a Citizen and Social Being
      IV. Choosing, Getting, and Holding a Job
   The MOST appropriate sequence is

   A. II, IV, I, III   B. IV, III, II, I
   C. I, II, III, IV   D. IV, I, III, II

8. Studies comparing the forgetting of completed and incomplete tasks tend to show that   8.____

   A. completed tasks tend to be forgotten more rapidly than incompleted ones
   B. incompleted tasks tend to be forgotten more rapidly than completed ones
   C. there is no difference in retention of the two types of tasks
   D. the inconclusive results that have been obtained make it impossible to generalize

9. Of the following, which is generally MOST conducive to the mastery of a skill?   9.____

   A. The practice of the skill in a daily routine
   B. Emphasis on speed rather than accuracy in early practice
   C. Overlearning
   D. Lack of emotion and pressure during practice

10. Degree of maturity, amount of previous experience, and motivation are all factors affecting the degree of _____ shown by a learner.   10.____

   A. intelligent activity   B. transfer of skills
   C. readiness   D. retention

11. Of the following, which one is of relatively minor effectiveness in determining the amount of transfer of learning from one subject to another? The   11.____

   A. degree of relationship between the two subjects involved
   B. methods used by the teacher to establish a relationship between the subjects involved
   C. amount of study time put in by the learner on the material
   D. ability of the learner to make generalizations

12. Where there are no adequate public facilities for the instruction of an intellectually disabled child who can reasonably be expected to profit from such instruction, the parent   12.____

   A. may keep the child at home until a facility becomes available
   B. may educate the child privately, deducting the costs from state and federal taxes as legitimate medical expenses
   C. may register the child in a class conducted by a parents' organization in the state, with the state paying tuition charges
   D. can apply for state aid under an appropriate section of the Education Law

13. Learning and maturation differ from one another as forms of behavior development in that the latter   13.____

   A. depends on special training during a critical period
   B. is continuous, while the former is not
   C. must be externally prompted
   D. appears spontaneously

14. The long retention of skills such as swimming is generally explained by reference to the   14.____

   A. law of multiple response
   B. law of effect
   C. effect of overlearning
   D. process of redisintegration

15. Which one of the following psychologists identified the five stages (sensorimotor opera-   15.____
tions, preconceptual thought, intuitive thought, concrete operations, and formal operations) in intellectual development?

    A. Edward L. Thorndike   B. Frances L. Ilg
    C. Jean Piaget   D. Arnold Gesell

16. A practical application of the *stimulus-response* theory of learning is BEST exemplified in   16.____
the classroom by the use of

    A. audio-visual aids
    B. experience charts
    C. developmental reading techniques
    D. teaching machines

17. Of the following, the use of the *conditioned-response* method of learning has been found   17.____
MOST successful in dealing with

    A. enuresis   B. epileptic seizures
    C. attitudes   D. reading disabilities

18. The type of forgetting in which people tend to forget the names of persons they do not   18.____
like is generally termed

    A. negative retention   B. repression
    C. proactive inhibition   D. retroactive inhibition

19. Experimental evidence suggests that the MOST effective learning and retention of mate-   19.____
rial such as poetry takes place when the material is memorized

    A. as a whole unit   B. word by word
    C. line by line   D. stanza by stanza

20. The MOST recent theories of the causation of reading disabilities stress as a major fac-   20.____
tor

    A. perceptual dysfunctions and lags
    B. lack of cultural stimulation
    C. minimal brain damage
    D. lack of parental interest and aspiration

KEY (CORRECT ANSWERS)

1.	D		11.	C
2.	B		12.	D
3.	D		13.	D
4.	C		14.	C
5.	A		15.	C
6.	C		16.	D
7.	A		17.	A
8.	A		18.	B
9.	C		19.	A
10.	C		20.	A

———

EXAMINATION SECTION
TEST 1

DIRECTIONS: Each question or incomplete statement is followed by several suggested answers or completions. Select the one that BEST answers the question or completes the statement. *PRINT THE LETTER OF THE CORRECT ANSWER IN THE SPACE AT THE RIGHT.*

1. Which of the following statements is TRUE?　　　　　　　　　　　　　　　　1.＿＿＿

   A. The goal of normalization is to allow one to do whatever one likes.
   B. Normalization involves making a person become normal.
   C. Normalization advocates that whenever possible, people's perceptions of developmentally disabled individuals must be enhanced or improved.
   D. Normalization advocates encouraging the developmentally disabled to be just like everyone else.

2. It is important to view the developmentally disabled as　　　　　　　　　　　2.＿＿＿

   A. helpless
   B. unable to make decisions
   C. deviant
   D. none of the above

3. All of the following would be considered good practice EXCEPT　　　　　　　3.＿＿＿

   A. providing residential services in the community, rather than in an isolated area
   B. placing residential homes next to rural prisons
   C. providing access in residences to accommodate those who are non-ambulatory
   D. avoiding excessive rules that tend to separate staff from residents

4. All of the following are true in normalization EXCEPT　　　　　　　　　　　4.＿＿＿

   A. family involvement in normalization is usually not helpful to achieving the goal
   B. clients should be involved, when possible, in selecting programming in order to develop independence
   C. program options should emphasize autonomy, independence, integration, and productivity
   D. it is a good idea when possible to have day programming located apart from the living setting

5. Benefits of normalization include all of the following EXCEPT　　　　　　　5.＿＿＿

   A. development of self-confidence and self-esteem in the developmentally disabled
   B. social integration of the developmentally disabled
   C. positive changes in societal attitudes regarding the developmentally disabled
   D. societal acceptance of deviance

6. All of the following statements are true EXCEPT:　　　　　　　　　　　　　6.＿＿＿

   A. Normalization means that normal conditions of life should be made available to developmentally disabled people
   B. Attitudes toward the disabled have a great effect on the way they are treated, and, consequently, on their chances for living a productive, normal life

C. It is highly unlikely that efforts at normalization will succeed in most communities
D. What is normal or typical in one society may not be normal or typical in another

7. In normalization, the means used to teach a skill are as important as the skill itself. In teaching adults, which of the following would be MOST appropriate?   7.____

   A. Working individually with someone after dinner in order to teach him or her how to brush their teeth
   B. Teaching pouring skills with sand in a sandbox
   C. Teaching how to button clothes by using a doll for practice
   D. Teaching how to tie shoelaces by first working with a baby shoe

8. Which of the following statements is TRUE?   8.____

   A. Residents' chore duties in a community residence should only change three times a year.
   B. Entrance into a community residence should be solely determined by an individual's need for a place to live.
   C. Using a task analysis for a client would involve breaking down a complex task into smaller, more understandable parts.
   D. Clients should be allowed to eat when and what they choose.

9. Select the one statement below that is NOT true of supervised community residences. A supervised community residence   9.____

   A. can provide short-term residence for individuals who need only training and experience in activities of daily living after a period of institutionalization or as an alternative to institutionalization
   B. can provide an institutional setting for those people who need it
   C. can provide long-term residence for individuals who are unlikely to acquire the skills necessary for more independent living
   D. usually requires staff on site at all times

10. All of the following are goals of community residences EXCEPT   10.____

   A. providing a home environment for developmentally disabled persons
   B. providing a setting where clients can learn the skills necessary to live in the least restrictive environment
   C. providing a setting where the developmentally disabled can acquire the skills necessary to live as independently as possible
   D. the community residence allows for the maximum level of independence inconsistent with a person's disability and functional level

11. All of the following statements are true EXCEPT: 11.____

   A. A community residence does not need to adhere to the principle of normalization in its physical or social structure
   B. The term least restrictive environment refers to an environment which most resembles that of non-handicapped peers where the needs of developmentally disabled persons can be met

C. A person's length of stay in a community residence extends only until a person has attained the skills and motivation to function successfully in a less restrictive setting

D. The purposes of a community residence may vary so that people with different ranges of abilities and levels of functioning may be served

12. All of the following statements are true EXCEPT: 12._____

A. Developmentally disabled persons residing in community residences must be afforded privacy, personal space, and freedom of access to the house as is consistent with their age and program needs

B. Transportation should be available from the nearest institution so that people in community residences have access to the community

C. The service needs of each person in a community residence should be individually planned by an interdisciplinary team

D. An interdisciplinary team should include staff of the community residence, providers of program and support services, and, if appropriate, the developmentally disabled person's correspondent

13. All of the following statements are true EXCEPT: 13._____

A. Supportive community residences are not required to provide staff on site 24 hours a day

B. Residents in supervised community residences may need more assistance in activities of daily living than persons residing in supportive community residences

C. An aim of a community residence is to maintain a family and home-like environment

D. Those living in a community residence shall spend at least three hours per weekday and one evening per week in programs and activities at the residence

14. In working in treatment teams, it is MOST important for team members to   14._____

A. communicate effectively with each other
B. keep morale high
C. attend meetings on time
D. enjoy working with each other

15. All of the following statements are true EXCEPT: 15._____

A. In teaching self-care skills, many tasks may need to be divided into sub-parts
B. Tasks which are easiest to learn should generally be taught first
C. Changes in routine are very helpful when teaching the intellectually disabled a new skill
D. The severely disabled do not learn as well from verbal instruction as they do from demonstration of a skill

16. All of the following statements are true EXCEPT: 16._____

A. It is important to evaluate the client's readiness to attempt learning a particular task before starting to teach the task
B. It is better to do a task for a client if the task may take much time and effort on his or her part
C. People generally learn faster when their efforts lead to an enjoyable activity
D. It is best when teaching a certain skill to begin with a small group when possible

17. All of the following statements are true EXCEPT: 17._____

   A. The expectations of a staff person of how well a client will be able to perform a certain task can influence daily living skills
   B. Environmental factors can influence daily living skills
   C. After seeing a skill demonstrated, a client should practice the skill
   D. A client will make a greater effort if he or she feels ill at ease with the instructor, and knows the instructor will become impatient if he or she continues to make mistakes

18. Of the following, the BEST way to teach a client an activity of daily living is to 18._____

   A. describe the steps to the client
   B. read the directions to the client
   C. break the activity into steps and have the client learn one step at a time
   D. have a client who can perform the task teach the client who cannot

19. All of the following are important steps in teaching a living skill EXCEPT 19._____

   A. defining the skill clearly
   B. determining the size of the skill
   C. breaking down each major step into substeps and sub-substeps as necessary
   D. rewarding the accomplishment of each step with candy

20. When teaching a daily living skill, it is important to keep in mind all of the following EXCEPT 20._____

   A. using concrete and specific language
   B. punishment can be a highly effective learning device
   C. matching the size of the skill to the client's ability level
   D. demonstrating what you want the resident to do

_____

KEY (CORRECT ANSWERS)

1. C	11. A
2. D	12. B
3. B	13. D
4. A	14. A
5. D	15. C
6. C	16. B
7. A	17. D
8. C	18. C
9. B	19. D
10. D	20. B

TEST 2

DIRECTIONS: Each question or incomplete statement is followed by several suggested answers or completions. Select the one that BEST answers the question or completes the statement. *PRINT THE LETTER OF THE CORRECT ANSWER IN THE SPACE AT THE RIGHT.*

1. All of the following would be considered qualities of a developmental disability EXCEPT the disability

    A. may be attributable to Down syndrome or autism
    B. has continued or can be expected to continue indefinitely
    C. can be easily overcome
    D. may be attributable to cerebral palsy or neurological impairment

1.____

2. The condition of autism

    A. applies to those people who have little or no control over their motor skills
    B. is hereditary
    C. is characterized by severe disorders of communication and behavior
    D. begins most frequently in adulthood

2.____

3. Secondary childhood autism differs from primary childhood autism in that

    A. primary childhood autism is more difficult to treat
    B. secondary childhood autism is secondary to disturbances such as brain damage
    C. secondary childhood autism is not as severe a disorder
    D. secondary childhood autism is less likely to interfere with behavior patterns

3.____

4. Which of the following would be LEAST adversely affected by autism?

    A. Interpersonal relations
    B. Learning
    C. Developmental rate and sequences
    D. Motor skills

4.____

5. Which of the following statements is NOT true?

    A. Cerebral palsy refers to a condition resulting from damage to the brain that may occur before, during or after birth and results in the loss of control over voluntary muscles in the body.
    B. Ataxic cerebral palsy is characterized by an inability to maintain normal balance.
    C. Someone with athetoid cerebral palsy would find it easier to maintain purposefulness of movements than someone with spastic cerebral palsy.
    D. Mixed cerebral palsy refers to the combination of two or more of the following categories of cerebral palsy such as the spastic, athetoid, ataxic, tremor, and rigid types.

5.____

6. All of the following are true about epilepsy EXCEPT

    A. epilepsy does not usually involve a loss of consciousness
    B. an *aura* often appears to the individual before a *grand mal* seizure occurs

6.____

C. people experiencing *petit mal* seizures are seldom aware that a seizure has occurred

D. status epilepticus, psychomotor, and Jacksonian are all forms of epilepsy

7. All of the following refer to neurological impairment EXCEPT 7.____

A. childhood aphasia is a condition characterized by the failure to develop, or difficulty in using, language and speech
B. epilepsy
C. minimal brain dysfunction is associated with deviations of the central nervous system
D. neurological impairment refers to a group of disorders of the central nervous system characterized by dysfunction in one or more, but not all, skills affecting communicative, perceptual, cognitive, memory, attentional, motor control, and appropriate social behaviors

8. Which of the following statements is TRUE? 8.____

A. Autistic children are below average in intelligence level.
B. All cerebral palsied persons are intellectually disabled.
C. Once an epileptic seizure has started, it cannot be stopped.
D. Autism is due to faulty early interactional patterns between child and mother.

9. All of the following are false EXCEPT 9.____

A. recent investigations have found that parents of autistic children have no specific common personality traits and no unusual environmental stresses
B. cerebral palsied persons cannot understand directions
C. it is not true that unless controlled seizures can cause further brain damage
D. the majority of the intellectually disabled are in institutions

10. In serving the needs of autistic persons, the one of the following which is usually LEAST important is the need 10.____

A. for training in social skills
B. for language stimulation
C. to deal with potentially self-injurious, repetitive, and aggressive behaviors
D. to teach skills that would improve intelligence

11. In serving the needs of persons with cerebral palsy, the one of the following which is usually LEAST important is the need 11.____

A. to experience normal movement and sensations as much as possible
B. to develop fundamental movement patterns which the person can regulate
C. for experience and guidance in social settings
D. to restrict their environment

12. All of the following statements are true EXCEPT: 12.____

    A. It is important that epileptic persons have balanced diets
    B. Pica, a craving for unnatural food, occurs with all intellectually disabled persons
    C. It has been projected that 50% of those individuals who have cerebral palsy are also intellectually disabled
    D. When working with the intellectually disabled, it is important to encourage sensory-motor stimulation, physical stimulation, language stimulation, social skills training, and the performance of daily living skills

13. When working with neurologically impaired persons, all of the following are true EXCEPT: 13.____

    A. There is usually a need for perceptual training
    B. It is important to keep in mind that an individual may know something one day and not know it the next
    C. It may be necessary to remove distracting stimuli
    D. It is important to keep in mind that neurologically impaired persons usually have substantially lower I.Q.'s than the average person

14. The developmentally disabled do NOT have the right to   14.____

    A. register and vote in elections
    B. marry
    C. confidentiality of records
    D. hit someone who teases them

15. Which of the following statements is TRUE?   15.____

    A. It is important for staff members not to make all of the choices for their intellectually disabled clients.
    B. Distraction is not a good technique to use when trying to channel potentially violent or destructive behavior to a socially acceptable outlet.
    C. Severely and profoundly disabled children do not appear to have a strong need for personal contact.
    D. It is primarily the mildly or moderately disabled child that exhibits the behavior usually associated with intellectual disability.

16. All of the following are causes of intellectual disability EXCEPT   16.____

    A. organic defects
    B. brain lesions
    C. increased sexual activity
    D. chromosomal abnormalities

17. An intellectually disabled patient who is *acting out*   17.____

    A. may be trying to communicate that he or she is physically uncomfortable or needs something
    B. should be ignored
    C. should be severely punished
    D. feels comfortable in his or her surroundings

18. In working with the developmentally disabled, all of the following would be appropriate   18.____
EXCEPT

    A. remembering that seemingly small things, both positive and negative, can be very important to the client
    B. allowing choices whenever possible
    C. maintaining a calm, level-headed attitude during an anxiety-producing situation will reassure clients and help them relax and feel safer
    D. after basic self-help skills have been mastered, it is not necessary to encourage further development

---

KEY (CORRECT ANSWERS)

1.	C		11.	D
2.	C		12.	B
3.	B		13.	D
4.	D		14.	D
5.	C		15.	A
6.	A		16.	C
7.	B		17.	A
8.	C		18.	D
9.	A			
10.	D			

EXAMINATION SECTION
TEST 1

DIRECTIONS: Each question or incomplete statement is followed by several suggested answers or completions. Select the one that BEST answers the question or completes the statement. *PRINT THE LETTER OF THE CORRECT ANSWER IN THE SPACE AT THE RIGHT.*

1. Marked improvement in a child's ability to draw a man over a brief period of time is MOST likely to be related to

   A. better social adjustment
   B. maturational effect
   C. the overcoming of a reading disability
   D. recovery from an illness

   1.____

2. Phenylketonuria, which is associated with intellectual disability, is a disorder of

   A. the reticuloendothelia system
   B. metabolism
   C. cerebral damage
   D. gyral defect

   2.____

3. A patient asserts, *I can't stand the agony I suffer when I go against my mother's wishes.* The therapist replies, *You really like to punish that momma inside of you for your dependency, don't you?*
   This response can be viewed as an example of

   A. reassurance   B. interpretation
   C. support   D. reflection of feeling

   3.____

4. A shy young first grade boy becomes extremely attached to his teacher. He brings her presents, asks her to help him with his clothing a great deal, and wants to sit near her all the time.
   He is MOST likely manifesting the mental mechanism of

   A. introjection   B. sublimation
   C. reaction-formation   D. transference

   4.____

5. The peculiarities of language behavior in the schizophrenic arise from his extreme need of a feeling of

   A. personal security   B. self-denial
   C. isolation   D. disarticulation

   5.____

6. The theory that psychical compensation for a feeling of physical or social inferiority is responsible for the development of a psychoneurosis is attributed to

   A. Adler   B. Horney   C. Freud   D. Sullivan

   6.____

7. Which of the following terms refers to the maintenance of stability in the physiological functioning of the organism?

    A. Functional autonomy   B. Canalization
    C. Homeostasis   D. Maturation

    7.____

8. Extensive studies of the personality and behavior of intellectually gifted children generally reveal that they

    A. are physically better developed on the whole than average children
    B. are more likely to be emotionally disturbed than average children
    C. are more prone to divorce in later life than average children
    D. more often come from homes in which emotional disturbance is present

    8.____

9. Expert opinion of professional workers with the physically handicapped indicates that a list of behavior characteristics would be headed generally by feelings of

    A. aggression   B. hostility   C. inferiority   D. courage

    9.____

10. Children with pykno-epilepsy suffer from _____ convulsions.

    A. diencephalic   B. visceral
    C. psychic equivalent   D. no

    10.____

11. Children with albinism and aniridia may read MOST comfortably with levels of illumination that, in relation to average levels of illumination, are

    A. upper   B. middle   C. lower   D. uneven

    11.____

12. Phenylpyruvic amentia has been traced to which of the following?

    A. Nutritional deficiency in the prenatal environment
    B. A single recessive gene
    C. Pathological nidation
    D. Effects of radiation

    12.____

13. Age of mother has been found to be MOST closely associated with the incidence of which of the following?

    A. Cerebral palsy   B. Cerebral angiomatosis
    C. Down syndrome   D. Hydrocephaly

    13.____

14. The so-called visual area of the cerebral cortex is located in the _____ lobe.

    A. frontal   B. parietal
    C. occipital   D. temporal

    14.____

15. Hypothyroidism is due to _____ in childhood.

    A. thyroid insufficiency   B. pituitary insufficiency
    C. thyroid excess   D. pituitary excess

    15.____

16. The inability to express oneself in words in spite of an adequate understanding and imaginal representation is called

    A. agraphia   B. aphemia   C. agnosia   D. aphexia

    16.____

17. Clara Thompson saw psychoanalysis as a method of therapy primarily designed to   17.____

    A.   give the individual new insights into his past experiences
    B.   help the individual master his difficulties in living
    C.   have the individual re-enact his relationships with his parents
    D.   strengthen the individual's ego defenses

18. According to Freud, the source of the large majority of the dreams recorded during anal-   18.____
    ysis is

    A.   a recent and psychologically significant event which is directly represented in the dream
    B.   several recent and significant events which are combined by the dream into a single whole
    C.   one or more recent and significant events which are represented in the dream-content by allusion to a contemporary but indifferent event
    D.   a subjectively significant experience which is constantly represented in the dream by allusion to a recent but indifferent impression

19. When an individual permits unpleasant impulses or thoughts access to consciousness   19.____
but does not permit their normal elaboration in associative connections and in affect, the psychoanalytic adjustment mechanism involved is

    A.   rationalization   B.   conversion
    C.   isolation   D.   introjection

20. In psychoanalytic thinking, repression can BEST be thought of as a(n)   20.____

    A.   attempt in projection
    B.   special type of introjection
    C.   reflection of acceptance of Id impulses
    D.   temporal form of regression

KEY (CORRECT ANSWERS)

1.	A		11.	C
2.	B		12.	B
3.	B		13.	C
4.	D		14.	C
5.	A		15.	A
6.	A		16.	B
7.	C		17.	B
8.	A		18.	D
9.	C		19.	C
10.	D		20.	D

———

TEST 2

DIRECTIONS: Each question or incomplete statement is followed by several suggested answers or completions. Select the one that BEST answers the question or completes the statement. *PRINT THE LETTER OF THE CORRECT ANSWER IN THE SPACE AT THE RIGHT.*

1. The behavior pattern considered to be deviate by clinicians is   1.____

   A. infractions of the moral code   B. generosity
   C. recessive personality   D. resistance to authority

2. A symptom of dementia praecox is   2.____

   A. tick paralysis   B. negativism
   C. extroversion   D. eremophobia

3. According to classic psychoanalytic thinking, the disorder MOST responsive to psycho-   3.____
analytic therapy is

   A. compulsive neurosis   B. hysteria
   C. narcissistic neurosis   D. obsessive neurosis

4. For the therapist, the MOST common meaning of resistance is that it is a(n)   4.____

   A. index of lack of suitability for treatment
   B. defensive attempt on the part of the patient
   C. reflection of superior therapeutic promise
   D. relatively rare phenomenon in psychotherapy

5. In a normal distribution, the percentage of children whose IQ's fall between 90 and 110 is   5.____
APPROXIMATELY

   A. 40   B. 50   C. 60   D. 70

6. The pioneer in mental diseases who was the first to make a distinction between emo-   6.____
tional disorder and intellectual disability was

   A. Kraepelin   B. Seguin   C. Esquirol   D. Galton

7. In psychoanalytic thinking, the term superego generally embraces the   7.____

   A. necessary social prohibitions as well as the higher cultural strivings and ideals
   B. unconscious strivings of the person as well as the ego-ideal
   C. unconscious reproaches of the person as well as the id strivings
   D. unconscious ego and its defense mechanism as well as the ego-ideal

8. A major contribution of Fromm to psychoanalysis can be considered to be his   8.____

   A. attempt to formulate the dynamics of orality and the concept of original sin
   B. belief that man has innate social feeling and a drive for perfection
   C. effort to relate the psychological forces operating in man to the society within which he lives
   D. effort to integrate the concept of psychosexual development with Rankian principles

9. José, a ten-year-old, has a hyperthyroid condition.   9.____
It is MOST likely that his behavior will be characterized by

    A. shyness, withdrawal, and reticence
    B. negativism, aggressiveness, and uncooperativeness
    C. placidity, passivity, and psychomotor delays
    D. restlessness, irritability, and excessive activity

10. The etiology of intellectual disability which is attributed to mechanical damage to the   10.____
fetus would be classified as

    A. exogenous   B. endogenous
    C. heterogenous   D. none of the above

11. The majority of children of intellectually disabled parents will have IQ's that in   11.____
relation to the IQ's of their parents are

    A. somewhat lower
    B. somewhat higher
    C. lower for boys and higher for girls
    D. lower for girls and higher for boys

12. Stuttering and stammering are MOST likely to develop between the ages of _____   12.____
years.

    A. 2 and 5   B. 6 and 9
    C. 10 and 13   D. 14 and 18

13. Most cases of stuttering are PRIMARILY the result of   13.____

    A. changed handedness   B. hereditary factors
    C. physiological defects   D. emotional problems

14. Anorexia is a condition which manifests itself in a loss of   14.____

    A. vision   B. appetite
    C. motor control   D. smell

15. Most differences in play activities and interests between boys and girls in the elementary   15.____
school years can PROBABLY be attributed to

    A. inherent biological differences
    B. inherent emotional differences
    C. instinctual influences
    D. cultural influences

16. The rate and pattern of early motor development of children depend MAINLY upon   16.____

    A. experience   B. acculturation
    C. maturation   D. training

17. Of the following, the BEST index of the anatomical age of young children is   17.____

    A. brain weight   B. ossification
    C. basal metabolism   D. dentition

18. When children of very superior mental ability are compared in size and weight with children of the same age whose mental ability is average, the former children are found to be 18.____

    A. above average
    B. average
    C. below average
    D. either above or below average, depending on the age level

19. The average child speaks his first word at _____ months. 19.____

    A. 6   B. 9   C. 12   D. 15

20. In Pavlov's classical study of conditioning, the unconditioned stimulus was the 20.____

    A. food   B. bell
    C. salivation   D. electric shock

21. Contemporary reinforcement learning theory suggests that the MOST effective learning takes place when correct responses are _____ and incorrect responses _____. 21.____

    A. rewarded; ignored   B. rewarded; punished
    C. ignored; punished   D. none of the above

22. According to the literature, girls tend to develop physiologically and socially about 22.____

    A. the same as boys
    B. one to two years more slowly than boys
    C. one to two years more quickly than boys
    D. none of the above

23. The mother of a newborn infant is told by her physician that she will have to have corrective surgery performed within the next 2 years. It is expected that the operation in addition to her convalescence will keep her away from her baby approximately one month. The period during which the separation would be LEAST advisable from the standpoint of the child's emotional development is between the ages of _____ months. 23.____

    A. 1 and 6   B. 8 and 16
    C. 16 and 20   D. 20 and 24

24. Of the following, the term to which empathy is LEAST related is 24.____

    A. sublimation   B. identification
    C. introjection   D. projection

KEY (CORRECT ANSWERS)

1.	C	11.	B
2.	B	12.	A
3.	B	13.	D
4.	B	14.	B
5.	B	15.	D
6.	C	16.	C
7.	A	17.	B
8.	C	18.	A
9.	D	19.	C
10.	A	20.	A

21. A
22. C
23. B
24. A

———

EXAMINATION SECTION
TEST 1

DIRECTIONS: Each question or incomplete statement is followed by several suggested answers or completions. Select the one that BEST answers the question or completes the statement. *PRINT THE LETTER OF THE CORRECT ANSWER IN THE SPACE AT THE RIGHT.*

1. A fusion operation upon the spine is often undertaken to correct

    A. pelvimetry
    C. epiphysistis
    B. paroxysm
    D. scoliosis

1.____

2. The treatment program for slipped epiphysis is MOST similar to the program for

    A. torticollis
    C. polydactylism
    B. Perthe's disease
    D. nephrosis

2.____

3. In general, the GREATEST difficulty is encountered in attempting to attain an intellectual evaluation of children with

    A. muscular dystrophy
    C. rheumatic fever
    B. cerebral palsy
    D. spina bifida

3.____

4. A physically handicapped child is enclosed in a box which enables her to stand and work. The child probably suffers from

    A. scoliosis
    C. spina bifida
    B. Perthe's disease
    D. cerebral palsy

4.____

5. Which one of the following types of cerebral palsy is characterized by uncontrolled movements, facial contortions and drooling?

    A. Ataxia
    C. Athetosis
    B. Spasticity
    D. Rigidity

5.____

6. Which one of the following is classified as a fissure of the brain?

    A. Maxillary plexuses
    C. Visceral cleavage
    B. Periphlebitis
    D. Parieto-occipital sulcus

6.____

7. Paralysis of corresponding parts on two sides of the body is known as

    A. diplegia
    C. monoplegia
    B. hemiplegia
    D. hemiparesis

7.____

8. Muscular dystrophy is a condition in which

    A. the cause is known
    B. there is apparently no hereditary transmission
    C. several members of the family are often affected in the same manner
    D. the juvenile type is rarely found in boys

8.____

9. A cleft of the vertebral column with meningeal protrusion is characteristic of

    A. Sprengel's deformity
    C. coxa vara
    B. scoliosis
    D. spina bifida

9.____

10. In general, children suffering from epilepsy should receive   10.___
   A. no psychological help if their seizures are adequately controlled by medication
   B. intensive psychological help regardless of seizure control
   C. psychological help only in instances where neurosurgery is indicated
   D. some type of psychological help in the form of psychotherapy, guidance, or counseling

11. Which one of the following diseases may result in brain damage?   11.___
   A. Poliomyelitis   B. Lymphadenoma
   C. Spondylitis   D. Encephalitis

12. Which one of the following involves the degeneration of parts of the brain, or spinal chord, or both?   12.___
   A. Schizophrenia   B. Spina bifida
   C. Multiple sclerosis   D. Pott's disease

13. Of the following, the disability with the BEST prognosis is   13.___
   A. Cooley's anemia   B. encephalitis
   C. hemophilia   D. slipped epiphyses

14. A child who has cerebral palsy has difficulty in keeping his paper on his desk. Which one of the following materials should his physical therapist provide to help him?   14.___
   A. A thick piece of oak tag
   B. A paper weight
   C. Masking tape
   D. A set of tacks

15. Excessive accumulation of cerebrospinal fluid within the skull is usually characterized as   15.___
   A. meningitis   B. microcephaly
   C. macrocephaly   D. hydrocephaly

16. Cerebral palsy is a term applied to a group of conditions having in common   16.___
   A. hereditary malformation
   B. trouble communicating
   C. microcephalic appearance
   D. disorders of muscular control

17. ADJUSTMENT TO PHYSICAL HANDICAP AND ILLNESS was written by   17.___
   A. Gesell   B. Michael-Smith
   C. Barker and others   D. Jersild

18. "Self-education" of children, accompanied by special emphasis on the training of senses, is MOST closely associated with   18.___
   A. Strauss   B. Cruickshank
   C. Montessori   D. Lehtinen

19. In the education of physically handicapped children, current theory favors stressing the child's   19.____

    A. special interests   B. motor abilities
    C. kinaesthetic sense   D. potentialities

20. The use of a board with holes and a rod as an adjunct to a teaching device suggests an adaptation of a(n)   20.____

    A. abacus   B. flannel board
    C. typewriter   D. marble board

21. Which one of the following would be MOST useful in therapy for a brain injured child who has a severe perceptual disorder?   21.____

    A. Bright pictures that tell a story
    B. Basal readers
    C. Educational games that teach addition and subtraction facts
    D. Three dimensional manipulative objects

22. In working with children with cerebral palsy who have problems in learning to read because of perceptual difficulties, the physical therapist should   22.____

    A. point to the words so that the child can follow the text more readily
    B. emphasize oral reading
    C. use a plain card to guide the child from line to line as he reads
    D. remove the neighboring children so that they offer no distractions

23. Research evidence indicates that handicapped pupils, as a group, show   23.____

    A. a higher incidence of below average intelligence than the normal
    B. an IQ distribution that is skewed towards the upper end of the scale
    C. a concentration of IQ's at both extremes
    D. an IQ distribution that approximates the normal

24. According to Strauss and Lehtinen, rote serial counting should be discouraged with the brain injured child because of his tendency toward   24.____

    A. perseveration   B. distractibility
    C. perceptual disturbances   D. hyperactivity

25. In general, children suffering from epilepsy should receive   25.____

    A. no psychological help, if their seizure are adequately controlled by medication
    B. intensive psychological help, regardless of seizure control
    C. psychological help only in instances where neuro-surgery is indicated
    D. some type of psychological help in the form of psychotherapy, guidance or counseling

KEY (CORRECT ANSWERS)

1.	D		11.	D
2.	B		12.	C
3.	B		13.	D
4.	D		14.	C
5.	C		15.	D
6.	D		16.	D
7.	A		17.	C
8.	C		18.	C
9.	D		19.	D
10.	D		20.	C

21.	D
22.	C
23.	A
24.	A
25.	D

―――――

TEST 2

DIRECTIONS: Each question or incomplete statement is followed by several suggested answers or completions. Select the one that BEST answers the question or completes the statement. *PRINT THE LETTER OF THE CORRECT ANSWER IN THE SPACE AT THE RIGHT.*

1.   Which one of the following diseases is always congenital?   1.____

    A.   Cerebral palsy   B.   Osteogenesis imperfecta
    C.   Rheumatoid arthritis   D.   Pericarditis

2.   Of the following, which condition represents a disturbance of the neuro-muscular system   2.____
    frequently accompanied by perceptual difficulties?

    A.   Perthe's disease   B.   Cerebral palsy
    C.   Spina bifida   D.   Talipes

3.   The following symptoms are noted in a group of children: enlargement of the calf mus-   3.____
    cles, difficulty in raising arms, afflicted shoulder and face muscles, waddling gait. The
    children are probably suffering from

    A.   spina bifida   B.   polio
    C.   muscular dystrophy   D.   Perthe's disease

4.   Of the following diseases, which one is hereditary?   4.____

    A.   Scoliosis   B.   Osteomyelitis
    C.   Hemophilia   D.   Chorea

5.   In which one of the following diseases is overweight frequently a concomitant?   5.____

    A.   Pott's disease   B.   Epilepsy
    C.   Slipped epiphysis   D.   Coxa Vara

6.   Hyperactivity is most apt to be observed in children who have   6.____

    A.   muscular dystrophy   B.   brain damage
    C.   ileitis   D.   rheumatic fever

7.   Three broad categories of physical disabilities - orthopedic, cardiac and chronic - are   7.____
    often used for convenience in classifying children in health conservation classes.
    The group below which best fits into the category of "chronic" is

    A.   rheumatic fever, muscular dystrophy, kyphosis
    B.   nephrosis, colitis, hepatitis
    C.   Friedreich's ataxia, osteomyelitis, torticollis
    D.   rickets, chorea, arthogryposis

8.   Congenital malformation of the brain is often associated with   8.____

    A.   hydrocephaly   B.   myelitis
    C.   varicella   D.   lupus erythematosus

9.   The use of an electroencephalogram usually proves most valuable in the diagnosis of   9.____

    A.   epilepsy   B.   osteoma
    C.   lordosis   D.   nephritis

10. Incontinence is most often an accompanying symptom of   10.____

    A. spina bifida   B. lordosis
    C. Friedreich's ataxia   D. Hodgkin's disease

11. A child with a positive EEG reading is likely to have   11.____

    A. asthma   B. rheumatic fever
    C. convulsive disorders   D. nephritis

12. Spasticity may reduce a child's ability to respond accurately to a therapist's questions   12.____
    requiring

    A. use of the sense of touch
    B. recall of prior learning
    C. knowledge of subject matter
    D. familiarity with domestic routines

13. Of the following, which child is MOST apt to encounter difficulty in handling spatial rela-   13.____
    tionships?

    A. The child with spina bifida
    B. The child with ulcerative colitis
    C. The child with Pott's disease
    D. The child with cerebral palsy

14. Which one of the following is characterized by involuntary, abnormal movements in the   14.____
    extremities?

    A. Myositus   B. Rheumatic fever
    C. Athetosis   D. Scoliosis

15. Of the following, the disease that is believed to have strong psychosomatic implications   15.____
    is

    A. colitis   B. diabetes
    C. anemia   D. hepatitis

16. Which one of the following is a congenital disease that involves the internal organs of the   16.____
    body?

    A. Cystic fibrosis   B. Nephritis
    C. Tuberculosis   D. Synovitis

17. Of the following disabilities, the one MOST likely to require a body cast is   17.____

    A. muscular dystrophy   B. scoliosis
    C. esophagitis   D. torticollis

18. Which one of the following conditions is CORRECTLY paired with an associated disabil-   18.____
    ity often found as a secondary defect?

    A. Cerebral palsy - hearing defect
    B. Chorea - visual defect
    C. Perthe's disease - speech defect
    D. Torticollis - poor coordination

19. In which one of the following pairs is it MOST difficult to arrive at a differential diagnosis?   19.____

    A. Encephalitis - meningitis
    B. Aphasia - brain damage
    C. Poliomyelitis - muscular dystrophy
    D. Hydrocephalia - microcephalia

20. Abnormal brain wave discharges are MOST characteristic of   20.____

    A. diabetes   B. epilepsy
    C. herpes   D. Hansen's disease

21. Most studies of children showing physical defects indicate that the incidence of defects is   21.____

    A. greater among intellectually disabled children than among normal children
    B. smaller among intellectually disabled children than among normal children
    C. about the same among intellectually disabled and normal children
    D. sometimes greater among intellectually disabled children and sometimes greater among normal children, depending upon the specific defect under study

22. Of the following, the one which does NOT represent a *major* problem for children who have physical handicaps is   22.____

    A. reduced capacity for affective relationships
    B. prolonged or frequent absence from home due to hospitalization
    C. differences in physical appearance from other children
    D. diminished opportunity for normal educational and recreational activities

23. In comparing physically handicapped children with physically normal children, it is correct to state that the physically handicapped child will usually be deprived MOST in which of these aspects of development?   23.____

    A. Social   B. Cultural
    C. Educational   D. Familial

24. The ability of physically handicapped individuals to cope satisfactorily with ridicule and other difficult situations   24.____

    A. depends largely on the attitudes of society toward the handicapped
    B. may be strengthened by special training in social techniques
    C. decreases as the handicapped individual matures
    D. is a function of the sex of the individual

25. Parents of physically handicapped youngsters often tend to overprotect their children. In most instances, this over-protection may be attributed to the parents'   25.____

    A. recognition of the child's greater need for protection
    B. projection of his own dependency needs on to the child
    C. unrecognized feelings of hostility and guilt toward the child
    D. wealth of affection which has too few outlets

KEY (CORRECT ANSWERS)

1.	B		11.	C
2.	B		12.	A
3.	C		13.	D
4.	C		14.	C
5.	C		15.	A
6.	B		16.	A
7.	B		17.	B
8.	A		18.	A
9.	A		19.	B
10.	A		20.	B

21.	A
22.	A
23.	A
24.	B
25.	C

———

EXAMINATION SECTION
TEST 1

DIRECTIONS: Each question or incomplete statement is followed by several suggested answers or completions. Select the one that BEST answers the question or completes the statement. *PRINT THE LETTER OF THE CORRECT ANSWER IN THE SPACE AT THE RIGHT.*

1. In selecting intellectually disabled patients for remedial reading instruction, primary consideration should be given to those patients who   1.____

    A. stand in the lowest quarter of the class on a good standardized reading test
    B. are recommended by the therapist as needing remedial reading instruction
    C. have a reading level below that to be expected from their mental ability
    D. show a high degree of motivation by requesting that they be placed in a remedial reading class

2. The LEAST common eye defect among children with reading difficulty is   2.____

    A. myopia   B. hypermetropia
    C. aniseikonia   D. strabismus

3. Otitis media is an infection of the   3.____

    A. nerves   B. middle ear
    C. dendrites   D. sclera

4. Poliomyelitis is caused by damage to the   4.____

    A. brain   B. musculature
    C. bones   D. nerves

5. Trachoma is a disease of the   5.____

    A. eyes   B. ears
    C. heart   D. bones

6. MOST orthopedic handicaps appear   6.____

    A. between birth and 5 years of age
    B. between 6 and 8 years of age
    C. between 9 and 12 years of age
    D. after 12 years of age

7. Muscle imbalance of the eye is called   7.____

    A. astigmatism   B. strabismus
    C. hyperopia   D. myopia

8. The child for whom education in a class for partially sighted children should be prescribed is one who has a visual acuity of   8.____

    A. 20/25   B. 20/40
    C. 20/50   D. 20/70

9. Among children with speech defects, visible body tension is MOST often to be seen in   9._____

   A. lispers   B. clutterers
   C. stutterers   D. lallers

10. The type of palsy which is associated with acute rigidity when the subject of reaching for   10._____
    something is

   A. atharoid   B. spastic
   C. ataxic   D. flaccid

11. A common congenital deformity in children is   11._____

   A. osteomyelitis   B. muscular dystrophy
   C. kyphosis   D. poliomyelitis

12. The following are four types of reaction of physically handicapped children to various sit-   12._____
    uations:
             I.   hysteria
             II. regression
             III. aggression
             IV. attention seeking
    Which two of these reactions are MOST closely related?

   A. I, IV   B. II, IV
   C. III, IV   D. I, II

13. Questions directed to professionals by parents of physically handicapped children most   13._____
    frequently deal with the area of

   A. methods of care and treatment
   B. institutionalization
   C. relationship of child to other persons
   D. causation

14. Large print reading materials and large charts are likely to be profitably employed for chil-   14._____
    dren with

   A. ataxia   B. multiple sclerosis
   C. ileitis   D. hemophilia

15. In order to prevent dropped wrists or uncontrolled wrists from inordinately striking the   15._____
    space bar of a typewriter, it is best to

   A. use a cover with holes above each key of the machine
   B. use a dowel for striking the keys
   C. have the typewriter rest in a sunken area into which it fits snugly
   D. bind the wrists to produce immobility

16. Socializing activities are ordinarily most difficult to achieve for physically handicapped   16._____
    children with

   A. leg fracture   B. muscular dystrophy
   C. colitis   D. asthma

17. A therapist of a physically handicapped girl discovers that her client's arms need immobilization during certain learning activities. The therapist should   17.____

    A. never use an activity that requires immobilization
    B. use a sling, twister, strap, or some other material to immobilize the arms
    C. suggest exercises to the child that will lead to better control over arm movement
    D. consult the child's physician for approval and recommendations as to methods of immobilization

18. Strauss and Lehtinen maintain that, with brain injured children, the form of writing that should be taught is   18.____

    A. cursive   B. manuscript
    C. block letter printing   D. colored manuscript

19. Of the following, the chief aim of language arts instruction for physically handicapped children is   19.____

    A. functional writing   B. curricular integration
    C. recreational reading   D. oral expression

20. The central focus of the arts and crafts experience for physically handicapped children should be   20.____

    A. development of technical skill
    B. making gifts for others to enjoy
    C. learning to handle new materials
    D. giving personal expression through an art medium

21. In a program of arts and crafts for the physically handicapped,   21.____

    A. the quality of workmanship is unimportant
    B. the aim is to teach leisure time activities
    C. the goals of achievement are the same as for normal children
    D. adjustments must be made in consideration of the child's disabilities

22. In organizing the work of a multi-grade handicapped class, the therapist should   22.____

    A. group the children according to their needs in skill subjects
    B. cover the minimum essentials for the several grades represented in the class
    C. find and plan for the average grade level of the class in all areas
    D. assign work on a "contract" basis

23. Of the following handicaps, which comprises the LARGEST group among United States school children?   23.____

    A. Orthopedic limitations   B. Lowered vitality
    C. Defective speech   D. Hearing difficulties

24. Which one of the following CORRECTLY describes the sequence to be followed in developing an art program with young physically handicapped children?   24.____

    A. Manipulative and exploratory activities; pre-planning; intuitive design; conscious design
    B. Manipulative and exploratory activities; intuitive design; conscious design; pre-planning

C. Pre-planning; manipulative and exploratory activities; intuitive design; conscious design
D. Pre-planning; intuitive design; manipulative and exploratory activities; conscious design

25. During the period of reading readiness and the initial reading period, the physically hand-   25.____
icapped child will be guided best to a recognition of words by

A. the use of picture and context clues
B. cutting out words from newspapers
C. structural analysis
D. the use of a class dictionary

_____

KEY (CORRECT ANSWERS)

1.	C		11.	C
2.	A		12.	C
3.	B		13.	A
4.	D		14.	A
5.	A		15.	C
6.	A		16.	B
7.	B		17.	D
8.	D		18.	A
9.	C		19.	D
10.	B		20.	D

21. D
22. A
23. C
24. B
25. A

_____

TEST 2

DIRECTIONS: Each question or incomplete statement is followed by several suggested answers or completions. Select the one that BEST answers the question or completes the Statement. *PRINT THE LETTER OF THE CORRECT ANSWER IN THE SPACE AT THE RIGHT.*

1. An ailment which does NOT occur as a functional disorder is

    A. tuberculosis
    C. hysterical paralysis

    B. stomach cramps
    D. stammering

    1._____

2. On occasion, Peter complains in school of dizziness. He appears to lose consciousness for a few seconds. During this period, he stops all activity and stares vacantly into space. His behavior is characteristic of children with

    A. grand mal
    C. myxedema

    B. petit mal
    D. encephalitis lethargica

    2._____

3. Anorexia is a condition which manifests itself in a loss of

    A. smell
    C. appetite

    B. kinaesthesia
    D. taste

    3._____

4. A disturbance of language perception and expression is called

    A. apraxia
    C. amentia

    B. amnesia
    D. alexia

    4._____

5. In oral reading, mixed lateral dominance is MOST often associated with

    A. omissions
    C. repetitions

    B. substitutions
    D. reversals

    5._____

6. Catharsis refers to

    A. emotional attachments
    B. a form of expressive therapy
    C. a sleep producing drug
    D. self-recriminating aggression

    6._____

7. Geriatrics is the study of the problems of the

    A. aged
    C. inmates of prison

    B. institutionalized insane
    D. behavior of infants

    7._____

8. An involuntary repetitive motor response primarily caused by emotional tension or problems is called

    A. apraxia
    C. tic

    B. palsy
    D. compulsion

    8._____

9. The patellar reflex can be observed on normal adults by tapping the

    A. elbow
    C. knee

    B. index finger
    D. heel

    9._____

10. An audiometer would be MOST useful in the detection of   10._____

    A. amaurosis   B. algesia
    C. alalia   D. anacusia

11. Persistent and irrational thoughts over which little mental control can be exercised are   11._____
called

    A. obsessions   B. compulsions
    C. retrogressions   D. symbolizations

12. Of the various basic instruments available for audiovisual instruction, the one BEST   12._____
adapted to work with an individual physically handicapped child is the

    A. tape recorder   B. filmstrip
    C. caliphone   D. 16 mm. projector

13. MOST helpful of the following gifts for the emotional and social growth of the physically   13._____
handicapped child is a

    A. set of jig-saw puzzles
    B. friendly, easily-cared-for pet
    C. simple science kit
    D. set of tempera paints

14. The "new" mental hygiene approach to disabilities gave great impetus to the establish-   14._____
ment of special educational facilities for the physically handicapped during the years

    A. 1866 - 1900   B. 1901 - 1918
    C. 1919 - 1950   D. 1951 - 1960

15. Improvement of conditions in the care and treatment of the orthopedically handicapped   15._____
first began to appear in the

    A. 14th century   B. 16th century
    C. 18th century   D. 20th century

16. The most common reaction of the physically handicapped child to separation from the   16._____
family because of hospitalization is

    A. depression   B. projection
    C. regression   D. sublimation

17. Research has demonstrated that the number of epileptic seizures may be decreased   17._____
through the use of psychotherapy.
One may conclude from such studies that

    A. epilepsy does not involve organic brain pathology
    B. epilepsy should not be treated chemically
    C. epilepsy involves an inherent personality deformity or disorder
    D. children may react to recognizable emotional crises with hysterical convulsions

18. The wearing of braces, crutches or casts would be apt to produce the most anxiety   18._____
among children between the ages of

    A. 4 - 6   B. 7 - 9
    C. 10 - 12   D. 13 - 15

19. Psychologists generally agree that when an emotional handicap exists in a person who   19.____
has a physical disability, the emotional handicap

    A.   usually stems directly from the physical handicap
    B.   is usually much the same in all persons with that particular physical disability
    C.   does not stem directly from the disability, but has been mediated by social variables
    D.   is apt to be extremely severe

20. In the development of desirable habits of oral usage, the program for physically handi-   20.____
capped pupils at all elementary grade levels should stress

    A.   a concern for correctness in oral communication
    B.   formal instruction in grammatical elements
    C.   individual practice on oral language errors
    D.   formal lessons on common class errors in usage

21. In general, physically handicapped children who find it difficult to make reasonable esti-   21.____
mates of the answers of problems before computing the answers should be

    A.   permitted to disregard estimating and to compute answers to all problems
    B.   given additional drill in written and computation
    C.   given practice with a larger variety of problems
    D.   asked to deal with problems involving simpler numbers

22. Musical toys and rhythmic instruments will have much appeal for the physically handi-   22.____
capped child if he first

    A.   uses them in group play
    B.   uses them as he desires
    C.   receives instruction in their use
    D.   sees them played by older children

23. Personality studies of physically handicapped persons and persons not so handicapped   23.____
show that

    A.   there is no significant difference in frequency of personality problems between the
         two groups
    B.   the most frequent personality deviation of the physically handicapped person is
         withdrawing behavior
    C.   persons with closely similar disabilities tend to develop similar personality struc-
         tures
    D.   nearly all physically handicapped persons exhibit evidence of personality difficul-
         ties

24. Of the following, which orthopedic disability gives rise to special educational placement   24.____
of the largest number of children?

    A.   Slipped epiphysis   B.   Multiple sclerosis
    C.   Lordosis   D.   Otitis

25.   A disease in which the muscles appear to be replaced with fatty tissue is   25._____

A. epiphysitis   B. kyphosis
C. muscular dystrophy   D. Still's disease

———————

KEY (CORRECT ANSWERS)

1.	A	11.	A
2.	B	12.	A
3.	C	13.	B
4.	D	14.	C
5.	D	15.	C
6.	C	16.	C
7.	A	17.	D
8.	C	18.	D
9.	C	19.	C
10.	D	20.	A

21.	D
22.	B
23.	B
24.	A
25.	C

———————

EXAMINATION SECTION
TEST 1

DIRECTIONS: Each question or incomplete statement is followed by several suggested answers or completions. Select the one the BEST answers the question or completes the statement. *PRINT THE LETTER OF THE CORRECT ANSWER IN THE SPACE AT THE RIGHT.*

1. Generally, slow learning is present in about _____% of people who suffer from Duch-enne muscular dystrophy.

   A. 30
   B. 50
   C. 70
   D. 90

1._____

2. When a particular behavior reliably occurs only in the presence of certain stimulus events, the behavior is said to be

   A. generalized
   B. indiscriminate
   C. internalized
   D. under stimulus control

2._____

3. In the placement/training phase of a habilitation program, which of the following actions is associated with the agency's habilitation strategies?

   A. Employing effective prosthetic/accommodation techniques
   B. Gathering longitudinal data on clients
   C. Seeking integrated living arrangements
   D. Updating intersector working arrangements

3._____

4. Support and follow-up for transitional employment placements generally lasts for a period of

   A. 30 days
   B. 90 days
   C. 6 months
   D. 1 year

4._____

5. In the human brain, functions associated with sensation generally originate in the

   A. cerebellum
   B. septum
   C. occipital lobe
   D. parietal lobe

5._____

6. The habilitation specialist's attitude of trust and respect in the presence of a disabled client is know as the

   A. accommodation gesture
   B. protective stance
   C. equity posture
   D. authority position

6._____

7. Which of the following is <u>not</u> one of the primary goals noted in the Developmental Disabil- 7.___
ities Assistance and Bill of Rights Act?

    A. Symptom alleviation
    B. Community integration
    C. Independence
    D. Productivity

8. The primary advantage associated with the use of functional definitions in relation to ser- 8.___
vice delivery and program design is that these definitions

    A. increase the likelihood that a person with functional limitations will be classified as
       disabled
    B. simplify administrative tasks such as budgeting and resource allocation
    C. fit in with an established state and federal framework
    D. encourage the individualization of program planning on a person-by-person basis

9. Of the following areas of life activity, in which is a person with epilepsy LEAST likely to 9.___
experience a deficit?

    A. Cognition
    B. Self-direction
    C. Economic self-sufficiency
    D. Independent living

10. Traditional techniques of behavior modification can be described as each of the following, 10.___
<u>except</u>

    A. dynamic
    B. insight-oriented
    C. systematic
    D. focusing on the past

11. A person's overall life satisfaction is categorized as a(n) _____ quality of life factor. 11.___

    A. physical
    B. cognitive
    C. material
    D. social

12. Which of the following behavior treatment techniques is probably LEAST appropriate for 12.___
affecting changes in the leisure skills of a mentally retarded client?

    A. Modeling
    B. Response contingent stimulation
    C. Physical prompts
    D. Verbal praise

13. Among mentally retarded persons, which of the following activities is likely to require the 13.___
greatest degree of intervention and rehabilitation?

    A. Gross motor control
    B. Housekeeping

C. Eating
D. Grooming

14. Autistic clients can be reliably distinguished from nonautistic retarded clients of similar IQ   14.____
    or mental age on the basis of each of the following, <u>except</u>

    A. cognitive test performance
    B. play patterns
    C. self-care
    D. language features

15. The goals of an individual habilitation plan include socialization, communication, and   15.____
    interaction. Which of the following instructional techniques will be most helpful?

    A. Providing opportunities for decisions and choice
    B. Developing a stimulus-response chain based on task analysis
    C. Teaching generalization of social exchanges to other persons and settings
    D. Presenting multiple training examples within individual sessions

16. Which of the following is a diagnostic condition that is most likely to result in sensory/   16.____
    neurological impairment?

    A. Multiple sclerosis
    B. Hydrocephalus
    C. Epilepsy
    D. Cerebral palsy

17. Which of the following skill domains is relatively strong among clients with spina bifida?   17.____

    A. Eye-hand coordination
    B. Mathematics
    C. Abstract reasoning
    D. Expressive language

18. Which of the following statements about generalized reinforcers is <u>false</u>?   18.____

    A. Their use takes place in a naturally occurring learning environment.
    B. Satiation is rare due to the wide variety of reinforcers for which they can be
        exchanged
    C. They bridge the delay between the performance of the behavior and the receipt of
        additional reinforcers.
    D. They are easy to store and dispense.

19. In the human brain, functions associated with emotions and their expression generally   19.____
    originate in the

    A. parietal lobe
    B. frontal lobe
    C. midbrain
    D. cerebellum

20. When selecting an instructional technique that will be effective with difficult-to-teach clients, it is important to choose the simplest possible successful strategy. The environmental components that need to be addressed include

    I.   the possible presence of some behavior that is incompatible with the task being taught
    II. the presence or absence of necessary prerequisite skills
    III. environmental stimuli such as the effectiveness of the instructions
    IV. the motivational system

    A. I and II
    B. II, III and IV
    C. III and IV
    D. I, II, III and IV

20.___

21. In the past decade or so, employment services to the disabled have generally changed in each of the following ways, <u>except</u> a(n)

    A. shift to public/private interfacing
    B. shift to separate work facilities for groups of disabled workers
    C. increased need for reportability focusing on person-referenced employment outcome data
    D. increased need for on-site evaluation, training and habitation practices

21.___

22. Approximately what percentage of cases of mental retardation have primary biological and medical origins?

    A. 10
    B. 25
    C. 50
    D. 75

22.___

23. During play sessions in which a retarded child is being taught appropriate play behavior, the child's first correct toy-play response after an average of 5 minutes have elapsed is reinforced. This is an example of _____ reinforcement.

    A. variable interval
    B. fixed interval
    C. variable ratio
    D. fixed ratio

23.___

24. Three Amendments to the U.S. Constitution have played an essential role in social change as it affects adults with disabilities. Which of the following is <u>not</u> one of them?

    A. Fifth
    B. Eighth
    C. Fourteenth
    D. Sixteenth

24.___

25. Overcorrection is a behavior reduction technique that includes the two components of   25.____
    A. response cost and modeling
    B. fading and extinction
    C. response cost and differential reinforcement
    D. restitution and positive practice

KEY (CORRECT ANSWERS)

1. C		11. B
2. D		12. B
3. A		13. B
4. C		14. C
5. D		15. C
6. C		16. C
7. A		17. D
8. D		18. A
9. A		19. C
10. C		20. D

21. B
22. B
23. A
24. D
25. D

TEST 2

DIRECTIONS: Each question or incomplete statement is followed by several suggested answers or completions. Select the one the BEST answers the question or completes the statement. *PRINT THE LETTER OF THE CORRECT ANSWER IN THE SPACE AT THE RIGHT.*

1. Which of the following is <u>not</u> an element of behavior analytic pre-vocational and vocational training?   1.___

    A. Acquisition, maintenance, and transfer
    B. Individualized training
    C. Qualitative description of behaviors
    D. Repeated assessments

2. According to the Developmental Disabilities Assistance and Bill of Rights Act, which of the following components is/are included in the definition of a severe and chronic "disability"?   2.___

    I. It is attributable to a mental or physical impairment, or a combination of both
    II. It reflects the person's need for a combination and sequence of special, interdisciplinary, or generic care, treatment, or other services
    III. It results in substantial functional limitations
    IV. It is attributable to substance dependence or adult-onset mental illness, or a combination of both

    A. I and II
    B. I, II and III
    C. I and IV
    D. I, II, III and IV

3. Which of the following is <u>not</u> a guideline that should be followed in the application of punishment to a developmentally disabled child?   3.___

    A. Avoid associating the delivery of punishment with the later delivery of reinforcement
    B. Apply punishment immediately following the behavior
    C. Punishment should be applied in graded steps
    D. Avoid prolonged or extensive use of punishment

4. Once a trainee has learned a new skill or reduced an inappropriate behavior, habilitation staff should consider the use of a(n)   4.___

    A. shaping sequence
    B. descriptive validation
    C. summative assessment
    D. intermittent schedule

5. In the human brain, functions associated with memory and the registration of new information generally originate in the   5.___

    A. parietal lobe
    B. temporal lobe

C. frontal lobe
D. hippocampus

6. The nutritional services offered to a person in a community contribute to the _____ of   6.____
   that person's quality of life.

   A. physical
   B. cognitive
   C. material
   D. social

7. The goals of an individual habilitation plan include generalization and mobility across   7.____
   environments. Which of the following instructional techniques will be most helpful?

   A. Determining the appropriate modes of client communication
   B. Sampling a range of relevant stimulus and response variation
   C. Building learning activities on the client's interest
   D. Simplifying the steps involved in a specific behavior

8. When using preference assessments for designing a habilitation program, each of the   8.____
   following is a guideline that should be followed, except

   A. if activities are presented to the person, all should be presented several times in
      different combinations
   B. program decisions should be made mostly on the basis of the personal interview
   C. each type of assessment should be done over a period of days
   D. equal attention should be paid to duration and quality of interactions

9. A client with muscular dystrophy is having difficulty feeding himself due to weakness in   9.____
   his arms. The first thing that should be tried is to

   A. raise the table or eating surface a bit
   B. fit the client with an elastic cuff that will hold a spoon
   C. feed the client for a while and see if he will attempt to self-feed again
   D. fit the client with special slings that will aid in feeding

10. Which of the following adaptations are most likely to be necessary for mentally retarded   10.____
    clients who take part in leisure activities?

    A. Personal training
    B. Environmental adaptations
    C. Rule or procedural alterations
    D. Material changes

11. Which of the following is an important consideration when developing a schedule of treat-   11.____
    ment sessions for an aphasic client?

    A. Aphasia, once corrected, is often followed by a period of dysfluency
    B. Aphasic persons communicate significantly better following periods of rest
    C. The utterings of an aphasic client are usually part of a syndrome
    D. Most aphasia is temporary

12. When a person leans to perform a desired response only in the presence of specific stimulus events, _____ occurred.

    A. generalization
    B. discrimination
    C. habituation
    D. shaping

12.____

13. When disabled workers lose their position in an integrated environment, it is usually because they

    A. were never very enthusiastic about the job
    B. have not been able to acquire the necessary skills
    C. did not receive adequate on-the-job support
    D. were unable to deal adequately with interpersonal issues

13.____

14. In behavioral modification, a generalized positive reinforcer may be exchanged by a client for a _____ reinforcer.

    A. conditioned
    B. negative
    C. backup
    D. contingent

14.____

15. A typical habilitation plan begins with a list of

    A. the client's goals as related to independence and integration
    B. the client's preferences and competencies
    C. a matching of the client with support services
    D. a summary of available resources

15.____

16. The primary disadvantage associated with the use of single-step behavior training is that the client

    A. is not aware of the ultimate goal of the behavior
    B. may experience difficulty transferring from skill training to the application session
    C. may not be provided with sufficient opportunities to practice discrimination
    D. does not have the opportunity to learn a skill intensively

16.____

17. Clients with _____ spina bifida are most likely to develop scoliosis.

    A. thoracic
    B. mid-lumbar
    C. lower lumbar
    D. sacral

17.____

18. Generally speaking, persons with a dual diagnosis are likely to be limited in life activity areas involving
    I. language
    II. independent living
    III. self-direction
    IV. learning

18.____

A. I and IV
B. II, III and IV
C. II and III
D. I, II, III and IV

19. When a client will perform a behavior better if she knows what the final product will be, which of the following instructional strategies is most appropriate?

    A. Forward chaining
    B. Response cost
    C. Backward chaining
    D. Full-sequence training

    19.____

20. Because of the limited amount of time generally available for behavioral skill instruction, habilitation workers generally make sure that the instruction is guided by each of the following principles, except

    A. strategies should involve action by the client and observation by the instructor
    B. the instruction should focus on functional attributes
    C. improvements brought about by behaviors should all relate to the client's quality of life
    D. the skills taught should relate to the person's life-aim goals

    20.____

21. When it occurs, a grand mal seizure usually lasts about

    A. 10-15 seconds
    B. 30-60 seconds
    C. 2-5 minutes
    D. 5-7 minutes

    21.____

22. Which of the following is common to virtually all language training programs for autistic or dual-diagnosis clients?

    A. generalization
    B. teaching in small progressive steps
    C. segregation into phonemes and morphemes
    D. discrimination

    22.____

23. Affective disorders are categorized as

    A. anxiety disorders
    B. psychoses
    C. syndrome-associated conditions
    D. personality disorders

    23.____

24. Which of the following is LEAST likely to be an area of deficit for a person with cerebral palsy?

    A. Independent living
    B. Learning
    C. Self-direction
    D. Self-care

    24.____

25. The focus of most community-living skills instruction programs for mentally retarded clients has tended to be   25.___

    A. telephone usage and money management
    B. language and socialization
    C. toileting and etiquette
    D. fire safety and mobility

————

KEY (CORRECT ANSWERS)

1.	C		11.	B
2.	B		12.	B
3.	C		13.	D
4.	D		14.	C
5.	B		15.	B
6.	A		16.	B
7.	B		17.	A
8.	B		18.	B
9.	A		19.	C
10.	C		20.	A

21.	C
22.	B
23.	B
24.	C
25.	A

————

EXAMINATION SECTION
TEST 1

DIRECTIONS: Each question or incomplete statement is followed by several suggested answers or completions. Select the one the BEST answers the question or completes the statement. *PRINT THE LETTER OF THE CORRECT ANSWER IN THE SPACE AT THE RIGHT.*

1. Intellectual disability is primarily a(n) _____ concept.   1._____

    A.   pharmaceutical
    B.   psychological
    C.   medical
    D.   behavioral

2. Trends which currently impact service delivery in habilitation programs include each of   2._____
   the following, <u>except</u> a focus on

    A.   outcomes and accountability
    B.   the natural environment
    C.   independent living in separate housing
    D.   rights and empowerment of persons to make choices and decisions

3. In general, individual habilitation plans should be reviewed   3._____

    A.   monthly
    B.   every 6 months
    C.   annually
    D.   every 2 years

4. Which of the following is a diagnostic condition that is most likely to result in physical   4._____
   impairment?

    A.   Down syndrome
    B.   Metabolic/immune deficiency disorder
    C.   Arthrogryposis
    D.   Bilateral blindness

5. A typical behavioral assessment concludes with a(n)   5._____

    A.   ecological analysis
    B.   contingency survey
    C.   list of behavior parameters
    D.   discussion of behavior change responsibility

6. Providing a client with work that is interesting, rewarding, and worthwhile is most likely to   6._____
   contribute to the _____ factors that foster well-being.

    A.   physical
    B.   material
    C.   cognitive
    D.   social

7. Of the following, probably the most significant trend affecting services for adults with dis-   7.___
abilities is

   A. evolving knowledge about particular medical or psychological conditions
   B. the involvement of family and friends
   C. the rise of the treatment/medical model
   D. the need for person-referenced outcomes

8. A 4-year-old autistic child who had just undergone cataract surgery needed to wear   8.___
glasses for nearly all of his waking hours, but consistently refused to do so, throwing
them aside whenever they were placed on his face. The habilitation staff decided to rein-
force the child's behavior in steps, rewarding him first for picking up his glasses, holding,
or carrying them; and then for wearing them for a few seconds at a time. Eventually, the
boy began to wear his glasses for 12 hours a day. The behavioral modification program
used by the staff in this case is an example of

   A. extinction
   B. shaping
   C. response priming
   D. negative reinforcement

9. Which of the following statements about transitional employment is <u>false</u>?   9.___

   A. Ongoing job-related supports are required by the disabled worker to maintain
       employment
   B. Extent of supports is flexible
   C. The work is in an environment where most people do not have disabilities
   D. Wages may be less than the prevailing or minimum rate

10. To teach an autistic client to use three-word utterances to label pictures or events, a   10.___
habilitation program should begin by helping the client to use _____.

   A. verb-adjective-noun
   B. negation in three words
   C. agent-action-object
   D. noun-verb-adverb

11. The two prime instructional strategies used in any behavior shaping program are   11.___

   A. discrimination and full-sequence training
   B. generalization and single-sequence training
   C. descriptive validation and response cost
   D. task analysis and instructional programming

12. Which of the following behavior reduction techniques generally involves the most punitive   12.___
strategies?

   A. overcorrection
   B. response contingent stimulation
   C. response cost
   D. differential reinforcement

13. Which of the following approaches would be most useful in assessing the behavior and characteristics of an inhabitant in a particular environment?   13.____

    A. Space coding
    B. Social ecology
    C. Organizational evaluation
    D. Person-environmental analysis

14. Approximately what percentage of all disabled U.S. adults are unemployed?   14.____

    A. 35
    B. 50
    C. 65
    D. 80

15. Sometimes, during the expressive language training of an intellectually disabled adult, imitative verbal responses are not learned through modeling alone; often, imitation must be   15.____

    A. generalized across major response domains
    B. shaped with physical prompts
    C. taught after functional or spontaneous speech is acquired
    D. placed into the demand/response mode

16. Generally, the training of receptive language skills in intellectually disabled clients has emphasized   16.____

    A. responses to sounds other than speech
    B. syntax
    C. verbal control of motor behavior
    D. reading aloud

17. Signs of tethering in a client with spina bifida include   17.____
    I. Back pain
    II. Pigeon-toed walk
    III. Progressive foot deformity
    IV. Spasticity

    A. I only
    B. I, III and IV
    C. II and IV
    D. I, II, III and IV

18. The use of intermittent reinforcement produces behavior that is   18.____

    A. easily produced upon demand
    B. more likely to produce satiation
    C. tends to be performed self-consciously
    D. more resistant to extinction

19. What is the term for a person's sense of where his/her body and limbs are in space?   19.____

    A. Kinesthesia
    B. Coordination

C. Proprioception
D. Dexterity

20. The federal law which states that all children with special needs should be placed in least restrictive environment possible is the

    A. Americans with Disabilities Act (ADA)
    B. Developmental Disabilities Assistance and Bill of Rights Act
    C. Individuals with Disabilities Education Act (IDEA)
    D. Rehabilitation Act

21. A person's _____ originates with the fluid in the canals of the inner ear.

    A. auricular
    B. proprioceptive
    C. tactile
    D. vestibular

22. When using the technique of a time-out from positive reinforcement in order to reduce a certain behavior, the most crucial consideration is

    A. the type of behavior (language and posture) used by the professional to direct the client to the time-out area
    B. whether the client loses access to an environment that is reinforcing
    C. the frequency of the imposition of the time-out period
    D. the duration of the time-out period

23. In evaluating a habilitation program, which of the following contrasts a service's outcomes with those of a comparison group to determine whether the service made a difference?

    A. Process analysis
    B. Outcome analysis
    C. Impact analysis
    D. Cost/benefit analysis

24. Which of the following is not common to all behavior modification techniques that are applied to meet the needs of disabled adults?

    A. The ability to reproduce responses at will
    B. Reinforcement contingencies to alter the frequency of responses
    C. The identification of observable responses
    D. The measurement of responses over time

25. An individual habilitation plan should
    I. identify which agency will provide each listed service
    II. have objectives stated in terms of emotional satisfaction
    III. always be in writing
    IV. include a statement of both short-term and long-term goals

A. I and II
B. I, III and IV
C. III and IV
D. I, II, III and IV

KEY (CORRECT ANSWERS)

1.	D		11.	D
2.	C		12.	B
3.	C		13.	D
4.	C		14.	C
5.	D		15.	B
6.	C		16.	C
7.	D		17.	B
8.	B		18.	D
9.	A		19.	A
10.	C		20.	C

21.	D
22.	B
23.	C
24.	A
25.	B

TEST 2

DIRECTIONS: Each question or incomplete statement is followed by several suggested answers or completions. Select the one the BEST answers the question or completes the statement. *PRINT THE LETTER OF THE CORRECT ANSWER IN THE SPACE AT THE RIGHT.*

1. Each of the following statements about the social reinforcement of desired behaviors is true, except that it   1.____

   A. is naturally occurring
   B. is automatically reinforcing
   C. doesn't interrupt the performance of the behavior
   D. is very easy to administer

2. In the currently evolving mindset among habilitation professionals, the one common element seems to be   2.____

   A. an emphasis on self-sufficiency
   B. a refocusing of service delivery from diagnostic categories to individual needs
   C. a universal set of professional standards
   D. a set of fixed service delivery principles

3. The basic underlying deficit of autistic clients is a(n)   3.____

   A. inability to perform basic self-care functions such as eating and grooming
   B. lack of gross motor control
   C. inability to exist independently of caretakers
   D. severe receptive and expressive language impairment

4. Which of the following is most likely to be a secondary condition related to the primary effects of a disability?   4.____

   A. Learning disability
   B. Speech disorder
   C. Dystrophy
   D. Intellectual disability

5. A person's self-help skills would most accurately be categorized as a(n) _____ of life factor.   5.____

   A. physical
   B. cognitive
   C. material
   D. social

6. Which of the following types of behavior treatment techniques is not widely used with clients who have a physical disability?   6.____

   A. Biofeedback
   B. Cognitive strategies
   C. Positive reinforcement
   D. Aversive control

7. Which of the following is a guideline that should be used in composing a client's behavioral outcomes?   7.____

    A. Specify the conditions under which the behavior will occur.
    B. Leave the date for final accomplishment open to allow for setbacks and adaptations.
    C. Avoid the use of contingency phrases
    D. Use the phrase "the client" or a suitable pronoun to avoid personalizing the objectives.

8. Which of the following is a diagnostic condition that is most likely to result in cognitive/developmental impairment?   8.____

    A. Fetal alcohol syndrome
    B. Spina bifida
    C. Hemiplegia
    D. Encephalocele

9. The main therapeutic goal for a hemiplegic client should be to   9.____

    A. teach the client to accomplish tasks with only one hand, by using substitutes for the other hand
    B. strengthen the leg of the weaker side
    C. outfit the client with the adequate number and type of prostheses that will be needed for basic self-care functions
    D. strengthen the arm of the weaker side

10. Research has shown that the prevalence of intellectual disability corresponds with age, with sharp increases until about _____ and a marked decline after _____.   10.____

    A. 12;15
    B. 18; 21
    C. 25; 35
    D. 32; 45

11. A serious health hazard of intellectually disabled clients is the ingestion of non-nutritive substances, known as   11.____

    A. mastication
    B. pica
    C. nostrum
    D. coprophagy

12. Among intellectually disabled persons, which of the following activities is likely to require the greatest degree of intervention and rehabilitation?   2.____

    A. Language reception
    B. Socialization
    C. Hygiene
    D. Physical coordination

13. For teaching toileting skills to autistic or dual-diagnosis clients, the best approach is
probably to use a combination of

    A. modeling and faded guidance
    B. overcorrection and response contingent stimulation
    C. faded guidance and extinction
    D. positive reinforcement and overcorrection

13.____

14. Which of the following is LEAST likely to be a reason why a person with neuromuscular
impairment might exhibit symptoms of incontinence?

    A. Kidney infection
    B. Shyness or embarrassment at needing assistance to use the bathroom
    C. Bladder infection
    D. Sphincter weakness associated with the disease

14.____

15. Clients with high blood levels of anticonvulsants are likely to display any or all of the following side effects, except

    A. personality changes
    B. motor slowness
    C. auditory hallucinations
    D. reduced intellectual function

15.____

16. Which of the following movements is generally possible for a client with L2 spina bifida?

    A. Hip flexion
    B. Hip adduction
    C. Ankle plantarflexion
    D. Knee extension

16.____

17. A client receives reinforcement every fifth time he drinks from his cup without spilling.
This is an example of _____ reinforcement.

    A. variable interval
    B. fixed interval
    C. variable ratio
    D. fixed ratio

17.____

18. Which of the following is a field of language teaching that attempts to account for language in terms of its uses in social contexts and discourse?

    A. Euphonies
    B. Pragmatics
    C. Mentalistics
    D. Sociolinguistics

18.____

19. An intellectually disabled client ruminates constantly throughout the day, despite verbal
reprimands from habilitation staff. Probably the best approach to eliminating this behavior
would be to

    A. begin providing positive reinforcement
    B. provide large quantities of food and allow the client to consume as much as she
likes

9.____

C. ignore the behavior as much as possible
D. offer the client only two meals, supervised, each day

20. From a habilitation planning perspective, there are significant trends among persons whose primary diagnosis is either intellectual disability, epilepsy, cerebral palsy, or dual diagnosis. Which of the following is not one of these?   20.____

A. There are significant group differences in the mean level of assistance scores on learning
B. There are few group differences in the level of economic self-sufficiency
C. There are significant group differences in the ability to live independently
D. There are few group differences in the level of self-care

21. For reducing the aggressive behaviors of autistic or dual-diagnosis clients, effective approaches include   21.____

I. generalized positive reinforcement
II. time-outs
III. extinction
IV. response contingent stimulation

A. I and II
B. II, III and IV
C. III and IV
D. I, II, III and IV

22. The federal law that requires an Individualized Education Plan (IEP) for school children who qualify for special education and related services is the   22.____

A. Americans with Disabilities Act (ADA)
B. Developmental Disabilities Assistance and Bill of Rights Act
C. Individuals with Disabilities Education Act (IDEA)
D. Rehabilitation Act

23. Of the following areas of life activity, adults diagnosed as intellectually disabled are LEAST likely to have deficits in the area of   23.____

A. language
B. self-direction
C. economic self-sufficiency
D. learning

24. For a young client with spina bifida, clean intermittent catheterization (CIC) should be performed _____ a day.   24.____

A. once
B. twice
C. 3 or 4 times
D. 5 or 6 times

25. Each of the following is a disadvantage associated with the use of categorical or diag-   25.____
nostic definitions in relation to service delivery and program design, <u>except</u>

    A. difficulty determining a general set of disabilities that need to be addressed
    B. overly rigid adherence to exclusionary policies
    C. insufficient acknowledgement of individual differences within a category
    D. lack of sensitivity in evaluation instruments

———

KEY (CORRECT ANSWERS)

1.	B		11.	B
2.	B		12.	B
3.	D		13.	D
4.	B		14.	D
5.	D		15.	C
6.	B		16.	B
7.	A		17.	D
8.	A		18.	B
9.	A		19.	B
10.	A		20.	A

21.	C
22.	D
23.	A
24.	D
25.	A

———

EXAMINATION SECTION
TEST 1

DIRECTIONS: Each question or incomplete statement is followed by several suggested answers or completions. Select the one that BEST answers the question or completes the statement. *PRINT THE LETTER OF THE CORRECT ANSWER IN THE SPACE AT THE RIGHT.*

1. It is GENERALLY accepted that, of the following, the MOST important medium for developing integration and continuity in learning on the job is   1.____

    A. day-to-day experience on the job
    B. the supervisory conference
    C. the staff meeting
    D. the professional seminar

2. Assume that you find that one of your workers is over-identifying with a particular client. Of the following, the MOST appropriate step for you to take FIRST in dealing with this situation is to   2.____

    A. transfer the case to another worker
    B. inform the worker that he cannot give satisfactory service if he overidentifies with a client
    C. interview the client yourself to determine his feelings about his relationship with the worker
    D. arrange a conference with the worker to discuss the reasons for her overidentification with this client

3. The one of the following which is the MOST likely reason why a newly-appointed supervisor would have a tendency to interfere actively in a relationship between one of his workers and a client is that the supervisor   3.____

    A. has unresolved feelings about relinquishing the role of worker, and has not yet accepted his role as supervisor
    B. must give direct assistance in the situation because the worker cannot handle it
    C. is attempting to share with his worker the knowledge and skill which he has developed in direct practice
    D. has not realized that immediate responsibility for work with clients has been delegated to others

4. A worker who has a tendency to resist authority and supervision can be helped MOST effectively if, of the following, the supervisor   4.____

    A. behaves in a strict and impersonal manner so that the worker will accept his authority as a supervisor
    B. modifies the relationship so that he will be less authoritarian and threatening to the worker
    C. gives the worker a simple, matter-of-fact interpretation of the supervisory relationship and has an understanding acceptance of the worker's response
    D. temporarily establishes a peer relationship with the worker in order to overcome his resistance

5. Before interviewing a newly-appointed worker for the first time, of the following, it is DESIRABLE for the supervisor to   5.____

    A. learn as much as he can about the worker's background and interests in order to eliminate the routine of asking questions and eliciting answers
    B. review the job information to be covered in order to make it easier to be impersonal and keep to the business at hand
    C. send the worker orientation material about the agency and the job and ask him to study it before the interview
    D. review available information about the worker in order to find an area of shared experience to serve as a *taking off* point for getting acquainted

6. In interviewing a new worker, of the following, it is IMPORTANT for the supervisor to   6.____

    A. give direction to the progress of the interview and maintain a leadership role throughout
    B. allow the worker to take the initiative in order to give him full scope for freedom of expression
    C. maintain a non-directional approach so that the worker will reveal his true attitudes and feelings
    D. avoid interrupting the worker, even though he seems to want to do all the talking

7. When a new worker, during his first few days, shows such symptoms of insecurity as *stage fright,* helpless immobility, or extreme talkativeness, of the following, it would be MOST helpful for the supervisor to   7.____

    A. start the worker out on some activity in which he is relatively secure
    B. ignore the symptoms and allow the worker to *sink or swim* on his own
    C. have a conference with the worker and interpret to him the reasons for his feelings of insecurity
    D. consider the probability that this worker may not be suited for a profession which requires skill in interpersonal relationships

8. Of the following, the MOST desirable method of minimizing workers' dependence on the supervisor and encouraging self-dependence is to   8.____

    A. hold group instead of individual supervisory conferences at regular intervals
    B. schedule individual supervisory conferences only in response to the workers' obvious need for guidance
    C. plan for progressive exposure to other opportunities for learning afforded by the agency and the community
    D. allow workers to learn by trial and error rather than by direct supervisory guidance

9. Of the following, it would NOT be appropriate for the supervisor to use early supervisory conferences with the new worker as a means of   9.____

    A. giving him direct practical help in order to get going on the job
    B. estimating the level of his native abilities, professional skills and experience
    C. getting clues as to his characteristic ways of learning in a new situation
    D. assessing his potential for future supervisory responsibility

10. Without careful planning by the supervisor for orientation of the new worker, an informal system of orientation by co-workers inevitably develops.
Such an informal system of orientation is USUALLY

    A. *beneficial*, because many new workers learn more readily when instructed by their peers
    B. *harmful,* because informal orientation by an undesig-nated co-worker can lead a new worker astray instead of helping him
    C. *beneficial,* because assumption by subordinates of responsibility for orientation will free the supervisor for other urgent work
    D. *harmful,* because such informal orientation by a co-worker will tend to destroy the authority of the supervisor

10.____

11. Of the following, the BEST way for a supervisor to assist a subordinate who has unusual work pressures is to

    A. relieve him of some of his cases until the pressures subside
    B. help him to decide which cases should be given the most attention during the period of pressure, and how to provide coverage for less urgent cases
    C. inform him that he must learn to tolerate and adjust to such pressures
    D. point out that he should learn to understand the causes of the pressures, which probably resulted from his own deficiencies

11.____

12. Many supervisors have a tendency to use case records mainly for the purpose of analysis of the workers' skill or evaluation of their performance.
Of the following, a PROBABLE result of this practice is that

    A. workers are likely to tie-in recording with supervisory evaluation of their work, without giving proper emphasis to their importance in improving service to clients
    B. the worker is likely to devote an inordinate amount of time to case records at the expense of his clients
    C. the records are likely to be too lengthy and detailed, limiting their value for other important purposes
    D. the records are likely to be of little value for administrative and research purposes

12.____

13. A common obstacle to adequate recording in a large social work agency is the fact that many workers consider recording to be a time-consuming chore.
In order to obtain the cooperation of staff in keeping proper records, of the following, it is MOST important for an agency to provide

    A. indisputable evidence of the intelligent use of records as tools in formulating policy and improving service
    B. a system of checks and controls to assure that workers are preparing adequate and timely records
    C. adequate clerical services and mechanical equipment for recording
    D. sufficient time for recording in the organization of every job

13.____

14. The one of the following which is NOT a purpose of keeping case records in an agency is

    A. planning   B. research
    C. training   D. job classification

14.____

15. When a supervisor is reviewing the records of a worker, of the following, he should plan to read
    15.___

    A. records of new cases only, following up each interview selectively
    B. the total caseload, in order to determine which aspects of the worker's performance should be examined
    C. those records which the worker has brought to the supervisor's attention because of the need for help
    D. a block of records selected according to the worker's need for help, and some records selected at random

16. The one of the following which is the PRIMARY purpose of the regular staff meeting in an agency is
    16.___

    A. initiation of action in order to get the agency's work done
    B. staff training and development
    C. program and policy determination
    D. communication of new policies and procedures

17. Of the following, group supervision in an agency is intended as a means of
    17.___

    A. strengthening the total supervisory process
    B. shifting the focus of supervision from the individual to the group
    C. saving costs in terms of time and manpower
    D. influencing policy through group interaction

18. The supervisor's job brings him closer to such limiting factors in the operation of an agency as faulty administrative structure, shortage of funds and lack of facilities, inadequacies in personnel practices, community pressures, and excessive workload.
    For the supervisor to make a practice of communicating to his subordinates his feelings of frustration about such limitations in the work setting would be
    18.___

    A. *appropriate,* because the worker will be more understanding of the supervisor's burdens and frustrations
    B. *inappropriate,* because the climate created will block rather than further the purposes of supervision
    C. *appropriate,* because such communication will create a more democratic climate between the worker and the supervisor
    D. *inappropriate,* because the supervisor must support and condone agency policies and practices in the presence of subordinates

19. A suggestion has been made that the teaching and administrative functions of supervision should be separated, so that the supervisor responsible for teaching would not be responsible for evaluation of the same workers.
    The one of the following which is the MOST important reason for this point of view is that
    19.___

    A. elements that confer on the supervisor a position of authority and power unduly threaten the learning situation
    B. teaching skill and administrative ability do aot usually go together
    C. a supervisor who has been responsible for training a worker is likely to be prejudiced in his favor
    D. performance evaluation and total job accountability should be two separate functions

20. In reviewing a worker's cases in preparation for a periodic evaluation, you note that she   20._____
has done a uniformly good job with certain types of cases and poor work with other types
of cases.
Of the following, the BEST approach for you to take in this situation is to

    A. bring this to the worker's attention, find out why she favors certain types of clients,
and discuss ways in which she can improve her service to all clients
    B. bring this to the worker's attention and suggest that she may need professional
counselling, as she seems to be blocked in working with certain types of cases
    C. assign to her mainly those cases which she handles best and transfer the types of
cases which she handles poorly to another worker
    D. accept the fact that a worker cannot be expected to give uniformly good service to
all clients, and take no further action

KEY (CORRECT ANSWERS)

1.	B		11.	B
2.	D		12.	A
3.	A		13.	A
4.	C		14.	D
5.	D		15.	D
6.	A		16.	A
7.	A		17.	A
8.	C		18.	B
9.	D		19.	A
10.	B		20.	A

TEST 2

DIRECTIONS: Each question or incomplete statement is followed by several suggested answers or completions. Select the one that BEST answers the question or completes the statement. *PRINT THE LETTER OF THE CORRECT ANSWER IN THE SPACE AT THE RIGHT.*

1. Of the following, the choice of method to be used in the supervisory process should be influenced MOST by the

    A. number and type of cases carried by each worker
    B. emotional maturity of the worker
    C. number of workers supervised and their past experience
    D. subject matter to be learned and the long range goals of supervision

1.____

2. In an evaluation conference with a worker, the BEST approach for the supervisor to take is to

    A. help the worker to identify his strengths as a basis for working on his weaknesses
    B. identify the worker's weaknesses and help him overcome them
    C. allow the worker to identify his weaknesses first and then suggest ways of overcoming them
    D. discuss the worker's weaknesses but emphasize his strengths

2.____

3. Assume that a worker is discouraged about the progress of his work and feels that it is futile to attempt to cope with many of his cases.
Of the following, it would be BEST for the supervisor to

    A. suggest to the worker that such feelings are inappropriate for a professional worker
    B. tell the worker that he must seek professional help in order to overcome these feelings
    C. reduce the worker's caseload and give him cases that are less complex
    D. review with the worker several of his cases in which there were obvious accomplishments

3.____

4. The supervisor is responsible for providing the worker with the following means of support, with the EXCEPTION of

    A. interest and advice on his personal problems
    B. instruction on community resources
    C. inspiration for carrying out the work of the agency
    D. understanding his strengths and limitations

4.____

5. When a worker frequently takes the initiative in asking questions and discussing problems during a supervisory conference, this is PROBABLY an indication that the

    A. supervisor is not sufficiently interested in the work
    B. conference is a positive learning experience for the worker
    C. worker is hostile and resists supervision
    D. supervisor's position of authority is in question

5.____

6. When a supervisor finds that one of his workers cannot accept criticism, of the following, it would be BEST for the supervisor to   6._____

   A. have the worker transferred to another supervisor
   B. warn the worker of disciplinary proceedings unless his attitude changes
   C. have the worker suspended after explaining the reason
   D. explore with the worker his attitude toward authority

7. Of the following, the condition which the inexperienced worker is LEAST likely to be aware of, without the guidance of the supervisor, is   7._____

   A. when he is successful in helping a client
   B. when he is not making progress in helping a client
   C. that he has a personal bias toward certain clients
   D. that he feels insecure because of lack of experience

8. The supervisor should provide an inexperienced worker with controls as well as freedom MAINLY because controls will   8._____

   A. enable him to set up his own controls sooner
   B. put him in a situation which is closer to the realities of life
   C. help him to use authority in handling a casework problem
   D. give him a feeling of security and lay the foundation for future self-direction

9. A result of the use of summarized case recording by the worker is that it   9._____

   A. gives the supervisor more responsibility for selecting cases to discuss in conference
   B. makes more time available for other activities
   C. lowers the morale of many workers
   D. decreases discussion of cases by the worker and the supervisor

10. The distinction between the role of professional workers and the role of auxiliary or sub-professional workers in an agency is based upon the   10._____

   A. position within the agency hierarchy
   B. amount of close supervision given
   C. emergent nature of tasks assigned
   D. functions performed

11. Of the following, the MOST important source of learning for the worker should be   11._____

   A. departmental directives and professional literature
   B. his co-workers in the agency
   C. the content of in-service training courses
   D. the clients in his caseload

12. A client is MOST likely to feel that he is receiving acceptance and understanding if the social worker   12._____

   A. gets detailed information about the client's problem
   B. demonstrates that he realistically understands the client's problem
   C. has an intellectual understanding of the client's problem
   D. offers the client assurance of assistance

13. A client will be MORE encouraged to speak freely about his problems if the worker   13.___

    A. avoids asking too many questions
    B. asks leading rather than pointed questions
    C. suggests possible answers
    D. identifies with the client

14. A client would be MOST likely to be able to accept help in a time of crisis and need if the   14.___
worker

    A. explains agency policy to him
    B. responds immediately to the client's need
    C. explains why help cannot be given immediately
    D. reaches out to help the client establish his rightful claim for assistance

15. It is a generally accepted principle that the worker should interpret for himself what the   15.___
client is saying, but usually should not pass his interpretation on to the client because the
client

    A. will become hostile to the worker
    B. should arrive at his own conclusions at his own pace
    C. must request the interpretation first
    D. usually wants facts, rather than the worker's interpretation

16. In evaluating the client's capacity to cope with his problems, it is MOST important for the   16.___
worker to assess his ability to

    A. form close relationships
    B. ask for help
    C. express his hostility
    D. verbalize his difficulties

17. When a worker finds that he disagrees strongly with an agency policy, it is DESIRABLE   17.___
for him to

    A. share his feelings about the policy with his client
    B. understand fully why he has such strong feelings about the policy
    C. refer cases involving the policy to his supervisor
    D. refuse to give help in cases involving the policy

18. Which of the following practices is BEST for a supervisor to use when assigning work to   18.___
his staff?

    A. Give workers with seniority the most difficult jobs
    B. Assign all unimportant work to the slower workers
    C. Permit each employee to pick the job he prefers
    D. Make assignments based on the workers' abilities

19. In which of the following instances is a supervisor MOST justified in giving commands to people under his supervision?
When

    A. they delay in following instructions which have been given to them clearly
    B. they become relaxed and slow about work, and he wants to speed up their production
    C. he must direct them in an emergency situation
    D. he is instructing them on jobs that are unfamiliar to them

19.____

20. Which of the following supervisory actions or attitudes is MOST likely to result in getting subordinates to try to do as much work as possible for a supervisor?
He

    A. shows that his most important interest is in schedules and production goals
    B. consistently pressures his staff to get the work out
    C. never fails to let them know he is in charge
    D. considers their abilities and needs while requiring that production goals be met

20.____

KEY (CORRECT ANSWERS)

1. D		11. D	
2. A		12. B	
3. D		13. D	
4. A		14. D	
5. B		15. B	
6. D		16. A	
7. C		17. B	
8. D		18. D	
9. B		19. C	
10. D		20. D	

TEST 3

DIRECTIONS: Each question or incomplete statement is followed by several suggested answers or completions. Select the one that BEST answers the question or completes the statement. *PRINT THE LETTER OF THE CORRECT ANSWER IN THE SPACE AT THE RIGHT.*

1. One of your workers comes to you and complains in an angry manner about your having chosen him for some particular assignment. In your opinion, the subject of the complaint is trivial and unimportant, but it seems to be quite important to your worker.
The BEST of the following actions for you to take in this situation is to

    A.   allow the worker to continue talking until he has calmed down and then explain the reasons for your having chosen him for that particular assignment
    B.   warn the worker to moderate his tone of voice at once because he is bordering on insubordination
    C.   tell the worker in a friendly tone that he is making a tremendous fuss over an extremely minor matter
    D.   point out to the worker that you are his immediate supervisor and that you are running the unit in accordance with official policy

1.___

2. The one of the following which is the LEAST desirable action for an assistant supervisor to take in disciplining a subordinate for an infraction of the rules is to

    A.   caution him against repetition of the infraction, even if it is minor
    B.   point out his progress in applying the rules at the same time that you reprimand him
    C.   be as specific as possible in reprimanding him for rule infractions
    D.   allow a cooling-off period to elapse before reprimanding him

2.___

3. A training program for workers assigned to the intake section should include actual practice in simulated interviews under simulated conditions.
The one of the following educational principles which is the CHIEF justification for this statement is that

    A.   the workers will remember what they see better and longer than what they read or hear
    B.   the workers will learn more effectively by actually doing the act themselves than they would learn from watching others do it
    C.   the conduct of simulated interviews once or twice will enable them to cope with the real situation with little difficulty
    D.   a training program must employ methods of a practical nature if the workers are to find anything of lasting value in it

3.___

4. In order for a supervisor to employ the system of democratic leadership in his supervision, it would *generally* be BEST for him to

    A.   allow his subordinates to assist in deciding on methods of work performance and job assignments but only in those areas where decisions have not been made on higher administrative levels

4.___

B. allow his subordinates to decide how to do the required work, interposing his authority when work is not completed on schedule or is improperly completed
C. attempt to make assignments of work to individuals only of the type which they enjoy doing
D. maintain control over job assignment and work production, but allow the subordinates to select methods of work and internal conditions of work at democratically conducted staff conferences

5. In a unit in which supervision has been considered quite effective, it has become necessary to press for above-normal production for a limited period to achieve a required goal. The one of the following which is a LEAST likely result of this pressure is that

A. there will be more *griping* by employees
B. some workers will do both more and better work than has been normal for them
C. there will be an enhanced feeling of group unity
D. there will be increased absenteeism

5._____

6. For a supervisor to encourage competitive feelings among his staff is

A. *advisable,* chiefly because the workers will perform more efficiently when they have proper motivation
B. *inadvisable,* chiefly because the workers will not perform well under the pressure of competition
C. *advisable,* chiefly because the workers will have a greater incentive to perform their job properly
D. *inadvisable,* chiefly because the workers may focus their attention on areas where they excel and neglect other essential aspects of the job

6._____

7. In selecting jobs to be assigned to a new worker, the supervisor should assign those jobs which

A. give the worker the greatest variety of experience
B. offer the worker the greatest opportunity to achieve concrete results
C. present the worker with the greatest stimulation because of their interesting nature
D. require the least amount of contact with outside agencies

7._____

8. A supervisor should avoid a detailed discussion of a worker-client interview with a new worker before the worker has fully recorded the interview CHIEFLY because such a discussion might

A. cover matters which are already fully covered and explained in the written record
B. make the worker forget some important detail learned during the interview
C. color the recording according to the worker's reaction to his supervisor's opinions
D. minimize the worker's feeling of having reached a decision independently

8._____

9. Some supervisors encourage their workers to submit a list of their questions about specific jobs or their comments about problems they wish to discuss in advance of the worker-supervisor conference. This practice is

A. *desirable,* chiefly because it helps to stimulate and focus the worker's thinking about his caseload
B. *undesirable,* chiefly because it will stifle the worker's free expression of his problems and attitudes

9._____

    C.   *desirable,* chiefly because it will allow the conference to move along more smoothly and quickly

    D.   *undesirable,* chiefly because it will restrict the scope of the conference and the variety of jobs discussed

10.   An alert supervisor hears a worker apparently giving the wrong information to a client and immediately reprimands him severely.
For the supervisor to reprimand the worker at this point is poor CHIEFLY because   10._____

    A.   instruction must precede correct performance
    B.   oral reprimands are less effective than written reprimands
    C.   the worker was given no opportunity to explain his reasons for what he did
    D.   more effective training can be obtained by discussing the errors with a group of workers

11.   The one of the following circumstances when it would generally be MOST proper for a supervisor to do a job himself rather than to train a subordinate to do the job is when it is   11._____

    A.   a job which the supervisor enjoys doing and does well
    B.   not a very time-consuming job but an important one
    C.   difficult to train another to do the job, yet is not difficult for the supervisor to do
    D.   unlikely that this or any similar job will have to be done again at any future time

12.   Effective training of subordinates requires that the supervisor understand certain facts about learning and forgetting processes.
Among these is the fact that people GENERALLY   12._____

    A.   forget what they learned at a much greater rate during the first day than during subsequent periods
    B.   both learn and forget at a relatively constant rate and this rate is dependent upon their general intellectual capacity
    C.   learn at a relatively constant rate except for periods of assimilation when the quantity of retained learning decreases while information is becoming firmly fixed in the mind
    D.   learn very slowly at first when introduced to a new topic, after which there is a great increase in the rate of learning

13.   It has been suggested that a subordinate who likes his supervisor will tend to do better work than one who does not.
According to the MOST widely held current theories of supervision, this suggestion is a   13._____

    A.   *bad* one, since personal relationships tend to interfere with proper professional relationships
    B.   *bad* one, since the strongest motivating factors are fear and uncertainty
    C.   *good* one, since liking one's supervisor is a motivating factor for good work performance
    D.   *good* one, since liking one's supervisor is the most important factor in employee performance

14. One factor which might be given consideration in deciding upon the optimum span of   14.____
    control of a supervisor over his immediate subordinates is the position of the supervisor
    in the hierarchy of the organization.
    It is *generally* considered PROPER that the number of subordinates immediately
    supervised by a higher, upper echelon supervisor _____ the number supervised by
    lower level supervisors.

    A. is unrelated to and tends to form no pattern with
    B. should be about the same as
    C. should be larger than
    D. should be smaller than

15. The one of the following instances when it is MOST important for an upper level supervi-   15.____
    sor to follow the chain of command is when he is

    A. communicating decisions   B. communicating information
    C. receiving suggestions   D. seeking information

16. At the end of his probationary period, a supervisor should be considered potentially valu-   16.____
    able in his position if he shows

    A. awareness of his areas of strength and weakness, identification with the adminis-
       tration of the department, and ability to learn under supervision
    B. skill in work, supervision, and administration, and a friendly, democratic approach
       to the staff
    C. knowledge of departmental policies and procedures and ability to carry them out,
       ability to use authority, and ability to direct the work of the staff
    D. an identification with the department, acceptance of responsibility, and ability to
       give help to the individuals who are to be supervised

17. Good supervision is selective because   17.____

    A. it is not necessary to direct all the activities of the person
    B. a supervisor would never have time to know the whole caseload of a worker
    C. workers resent too much help from a supervisor
    D. too much reading is a waste of valuable time

18. An important administrative problem is how precisely to define the limits of authority that   18.____
    is delegated to subordinate supervisors.
    Such definition of limits of authority should be

    A. as precise as possible and practicable in all areas
    B. as precise as possible and practicable in areas of function, but should allow con-
       siderable flexibility in the area of personnel management
    C. as precise as possible and practicable in the area
    D. of personnel management, but should allow considerable flexibility in the areas of
       function
    E. in general terms so as to allow considerable flexibility both in the areas of function
       and in the areas of personnel management

19. Experts in the field of personnel relations feel that it is generally a bad practice for subor-   19.____
dinate employees to become aware of pending or contemplated changes in policy or
organizational set-up via the *grapevine* CHIEFLY because

    A. evidence that one or more responsible officials have proved untrustworthy will
undermine confidence in the agency

    B. the information disseminated by this method is seldom entirely accurate and gen-
erally spreads needless unrest among the subordinate staff

    C. the subordinate staff may conclude that the administration feels the staff cannot be
trusted with the true information

    D. the subordinate staff may conclude that the administration lacks the courage to
make an unpopular announcement through official channels

20. Supervision is subject to many interpretations, depending on the area in which it func-   20.____
tions.
Of the following, the statement which represents the MOST appropriate meaning of
supervision as it is known in social work practice is that it

    A. is a leadership process for the development of new leaders

    B. is an educational and administrative process aimed at teaching personnel the goal
of improved service to the client

    C. is an activity aimed chiefly at insuring that workers will adhere to all agency direc-
tives

    D. provides the opportunity for administration to secure staff reaction to agency poli-
cies

21. A supervisor may utilize various methods in the supervisory process.   21.____
The one of the following upon which sound supervisory practice rests in the selection
of supervisory techniques is

    A. an estimate of the worker arrived at through current and past evaluation of perfor-
mance as well as through worker's participation

    B. the previous supervisor's evaluation and recommendation

    C. the worker's expression of his personal preference for certain types of experience

    D. the amount of time available to supervisor and supervisee

22. It is the practice of some supervisors, when they believe that it would be desirable for a   22.____
subordinate to take a particular action in a case, to inform the subordinate of this in the
form of a suggestion rather than in the form of a direct order.
In general, this method of getting a subordinate to take the desired action is

    A. *inadvisable;* it may create in the mind of the subordinate the impression that the
supervisor is uncertain about the efficacy of her plan and is trying to avoid whatever responsibility she may have in resolving the case

    B. *advisable;* it provides the subordinate with the maximum opportunity to use her
own judgment in handling the case

    C. *inadvisable;* it provides the subordinate with no clear-cut direction and, therefore, is
likely to leave her with a feeling of uncertainty and frustration

    D. *advisable;* it presents the supervisor's view in a manner which will be most likely to
evoke the subordinate's cooperation

23. A veteran supervisor noticed that one of her workers of average ability had begun developing some bad work habits, becoming especially careless in her recordkeeping. After reprimand from the supervisor, the investigator corrected her errors and has been doing satisfactory work since then.
For the supervisor to keep referring to this period of poor work during her weekly conferences with this employee would *generally* be considered poor personnel practice CHIEFLY because

    A. praise rather than criticism is generally the best method to use in improving the work of an unsatisfactory worker
    B. the supervisor cannot know whether the employee's errors will follow an established pattern
    C. the fault which evoked the original negative criticism no longer exists
    D. this would tend to frustrate the worker by making her strive overly hard to reach a level of productivity which is beyond her ability to achieve

23.____

24. Assume that you are now a supervisor in a specific unit. Two experienced investigators in your unit, both of whom do above average work, have for some time not gotten along with each other for personal reasons. Their attitude toward one another has suddenly become hostile and noisy disagreement has taken place in the office.
The BEST action for you to take FIRST in this situation is to

    A. transfer one of the two investigators to another unit where contact with the other investigator will be unnecessary
    B. discuss the problem with the two investigators together, insisting that they confide in you and tell you the cause of their mutual antagonism
    C. confer with the two investigators separately, pointing out to each the need to adopt an adult professional attitude with respect to their on-the-job relations
    D. advise the two investigators that should the situation grow worse, disciplinary action will be considered

24.____

25. It has long been recognized that relationships exist between worker morale and working conditions. The one of the following which BEST clarifies these existing relationships is that morale is

    A. affected for better or for worse in direct relationship to the magnitude of the changes in working conditions for better or worse
    B. better when working conditions are better
    C. little affected by working conditions so long as the working conditions do not approach the intolerable
    D. more affected by the degree of interest shown in providing good working conditions than by the actual conditions and may, perversely, be highest when working conditions are worst

25.____

KEY (CORRECT ANSWERS)

1.	A		11.	D
2.	D		12.	A
3.	B		13.	C
4.	A		14.	D
5.	D		15.	A
6.	D		16.	D
7.	B		17.	A
8.	C		18.	A
9.	A		19.	B
10.	C		20.	B

21.	A
22.	D
23.	C
24.	C
25.	D

———

PREPARING WRITTEN MATERIAL

PARAGRAPH REARRANGEMENT
COMMENTARY

The sentences which follow are in scrambled order. You are to rearrange them in proper order and indicate the letter choice containing the correct answer at the space at the right.

Each group of sentences in this section is actually a paragraph presented in scrambled order. Each sentence in the group has a place in that paragraph; no sentence is to be left out. You are to read each group of sentences and decide upon the best order in which to put the sentences so as to form as well-organized paragraph.

The questions in this section measure the ability to solve a problem when all the facts relevant to its solution are not given.

More specifically, certain positions of responsibility and authority require the employee to discover connections between events sometimes, apparently, unrelated. In order to do this, the employee will find it necessary to correctly infer that unspecified events have probably occurred or are likely to occur. This ability becomes especially important when action must be taken on incomplete information.

Accordingly, these questions require competitors to choose among several suggested alternatives, each of which presents a different sequential arrangement of the events. Competitors must choose the MOST logical of the suggested sequences.

In order to do so, they may be required to draw on general knowledge to infer missing concepts or events that are essential to sequencing the given events. Competitors should be careful to infer only what is essential to the sequence. The plausibility of the wrong alternatives will always require the inclusion of unlikely events or of additional chains of events which are NOT essential to sequencing the given events.

It's very important to remember that you are looking for the best of the four possible choices, and that the best choice of all may not even be one of the answers you're given to choose from.

There is no one right way to these problems. Many people have found it helpful to first write out the order of the sentences, as they would have arranged them, on their scrap paper before looking at the possible answers. If their optimum answer is there, this can save them some time. If it isn't, this method can still give insight into solving the problem. Others find it most helpful to just go through each of the possible choices, contrasting each as they go along. You should use whatever method feels comfortable, and works, for you.

While most of these types of questions are not that difficult, we've added a higher percentage of the difficult type, just to give you more practice. Usually there are only one or two questions on this section that contain such subtle distinctions that you're unable to answer confidently, and you then may find yourself stuck deciding between two possible choices, neither of which you're sure about.

EXAMINATION SECTION
TEST 1

DIRECTIONS: The sentences that follow are in scrambled order. You are to rearrange them in proper order and indicate the letter choice containing the correct answer. *PRINT THE LETTER OF THE CORRECT ANSWER IN THE SPACE AT THE RIGHT.*

1. Below are four statements labeled W., X., Y., and Z.   1.____
    W.   He was a strict and fanatic drillmaster.
    X.   The word is always used in a derogatory sense and generally shows resentment and anger on the part of the user.
    Y.   It is from the name of this Frenchman that we derive our English word, martinet.
    Z.   Jean Martinet was the Inspector-General of Infantry during the reign of King Louis XIV.
    The *PROPER* order in which these sentences should be placed in a paragraph is:

    A. X, Z, W, Y   B. X, Z, Y, W   C. Z, W, Y, X   D. Z, Y, W, X

2. In the following paragraph, the sentences which are numbered, have been jumbled.   2.____
    1.   Since then it has undergone changes.
    2.   It was incorporated in 1955 under the laws of the State of New York.
    3.   Its primary purpose, a cleaner city, has, however, remained the same.
    4.   The Citizens Committee works in cooperation with the Mayor's Inter-departmental Committee for a Clean City.
    The order in which these sentences should be arranged to form a well-organized paragraph is:

    A. 2, 4, 1, 3   B. 3, 4, 1, 2   C. 4, 2, 1, 3   D. 4, 3, 2, 1

Questions 3-5.

DIRECTIONS: The sentences listed below are part of a meaningful paragraph but they are not given in their proper order. You are to decide what would be the *best order* in which to put the sentences so as to form a well-organized paragraph. Each sentence has a place in the paragraph; there are no extra sentences. You are then to answer questions 3 to 5 inclusive on the basis of your rearrangements of these secrambled sentences into a properly organized paragraph.

In 1887 some insurance companies organized an Inspection Department to advise their clients on all phases of fire prevention and protection. Probably this has been due to the smaller annual fire losses in Great Britain than in the United States. It tests various fire prevention devices and appliances and determines manufacturing hazards and their safeguards. Fire research began earlier in the United States and is more advanced than in Great Britain. Later they established a laboratory specializing in electrical, mechanical, hydraulic, and chemical fields.

3. When the five sentences are arranged in proper order, the paragraph starts with the sentence which begins

    3.____

  A. "In 1887..."   B. "Probably this ..."   C. "It tests ..."
  D. "Fire research ..."   E. "Later they ..."

4. In the last sentence listed above, "they" refers to

    4.____

  A. insurance companies
  B. the United States and Great Britain
  C. the Inspection Department
  D. clients
  E. technicians

5. When the above paragraph is properly arranged, it ends with the words

    5.____

  A. "... and protection."   B. "... the United States."
  C. "... their safeguards."   D. "... in Great Britain."
  E. "... chemical fields."

KEY (CORRECT ANSWERS)

1. C
2. C
3. D
4. A
5. C

TEST 2

DIRECTIONS: In each of the questions numbered 1 through 5, several sentences are given. For each question, choose as your answer the group of numbers that represents the *most logical* order of these sentences if they were arranged in paragraph form. *PRINT THE LETTER OF THE CORRECT ANSWER IN THE SPACE AT THE RIGHT.*

1. 1. It is established when one shows that the landlord has prevented the tenant's enjoyment of his interest in the property leased.
   2. Constructive eviction is the result of a breach of the covenant of quiet enjoyment implied in all leases.
   3. In some parts of the United States, it is not complete until the tenant vacates within a reasonable time.
   4. Generally, the acts must be of such serious and permanent character as to deny the tenant the enjoyment of his possessing rights.
   5. In this event, upon abandonment of the premises, the tenant's liability for that ceases.

   The CORRECT answer is:

   A. 2, 1, 4, 3, 5   B. 5, 2, 3, 1, 4   C. 4, 3, 1, 2, 5
   D. 1, 3, 5, 4, 2   1.____

2. 1. The powerlessness before private and public authorities that is the typical experience of the slum tenant is reminiscent of the situation of blue-collar workers all through the nineteenth century.
   2. Similarly, in recent years, this chapter of history has been reopened by anti-poverty groups which have attempted to organize slum tenants to enable them to bargain collectively with their landlords about the conditions of their tenancies.
   3. It is familiar history that many of the workers remedied their condition by joining together and presenting their demands collectively.
   4. Like the workers, tenants are forced by the conditions of modern life into substantial dependence on these who possess great political arid economic power.
   5. What's more, the very fact of dependence coupled with an absence of education and self-confidence makes them hesitant and unable to stand up for what they need from those in power.

   The CORRECT answer is:

   A. 5, 4, 1, 2, 3   B. 2, 3, 1, 5, 4   C. 3, 1, 5, 4, 2
   D. 1, 4, 5, 3, 2   2.____

3. 1. A railroad, for example, when not acting as a common carrier may contract; away responsibility for its own negligence.
   2. As to a landlord, however, no decision has been found relating to the legal effect of a clause shifting the statutory duty of repair to the tenant.
   3. The courts have not passed on the validity of clauses relieving the landlord of this duty and liability.
   4. They have, however, upheld the validity of exculpatory clauses in other types of contracts.
   5. Housing regulations impose a duty upon the landlord to maintain leased premises in safe condition.

                                                                        3.____

6. As another example, a bailee may limit his liability except for gross negligence, willful acts, or fraud.

The CORRECT answer is:

A. 2, 1, 6, 4, 3, 5   B. 1, 3, 4, 5, 6, 2   C. 3, 5, 1, 4, 2, 6
D. 5, 3, 4, 1, 6, 2

4.   1. Since there are only samples in the building, retail or consumer sales are generally eschewed by mart occupants, and,in some instances, rigid controls are maintained to limit entrance to the mart only to those persons engaged in retailing.   4.____
    2. Since World War I, in many larger cities, there has developed a new type of property, called the mart building.
    3. It can, therefore, be used by wholesalers and jobbers for the display of sample merchandise.
    4. This type of building is most frequently a multi-storied, finished interior property which is a cross between a retail arcade and a loft building.
    5. This limitation enables the mart occupants to ship the orders from another location after the retailer or dealer makes his selection from the samples.

The CORRECT answer is:

A. 2, 4, 3, 1, 5   B. 4, 3, 5, 1, 2   C. 1, 3, 2, 4, 5
D. 1, 4, 2, 3, 5

5.   1. In general, staff-line friction reduces the distinctive contribution of staff personnel.   5.____
    2. The conflicts, however, introduce an uncontrolled element into the managerial system.
    3. On the other hand, the natural resistance of the line to staff innovations probably usefully restrains over-eager efforts to apply untested procedures on a large scale.
    4. Under such conditions, it is difficult to know when valuable ideas are being sacrificed.
    5. The relatively weak position of staff, requiring accommodation to the line, tends to restrict their ability to engage .in free, experimental innovation.

The CORRECT answer is:

A. 4, 2, 3, 1, 3   B. 1, 5, 3, 2, 4   C. 5, 3, 1, 2, 4
D. 2, 1, 4, 5, 3

———

KEY (CORRECT ANSWERS)

1. A
2. D
3. D
4. A
5. B

———

TEST 3

DIRECTIONS: Questions 1 through 4 consist of six sentences which can be arranged in a logical sequence. For each question, select the choice which places the numbered sentences in the *most logical* sequence. *PRINT THE LETTER OF THE CORRECT ANSWER IN THE SPACE AT THE RIGHT.*

1.   1. The burden of proof as to each issue is determined before trial and remains upon the same party throughout the trial.
       2. The jury is at liberty to believe one witness' testimony as against a number of contradictory witnesses.
       3. In a civil case, the party bearing the burden of proof is required to prove his contention by a fair preponderance of the evidence.
       4. However, it must be noted that a fair preponderance of evidence does not necessarily mean a greater number of witnesses.
       5. The burden of proof is the burden which rests upon one of the parties to an action to persuade the trier of the facts, generally the jury, that a proposition he asserts is true.
       6. If the evidence is equally balanced, or if it leaves the jury in such doubt as to be unable to decide the controversy either way, judgment must be given against the party upon whom the burden of proof rests.

The CORRECT answer is:

  A. 3, 2, 5, 4, 1, 6   B. 1, 2, 6, 5, 3, 4   C. 3, 4, 5, 1, 2, 6
  D. 5, 1, 3, 6, 4, 2

1.____

2.   1. If a parent is without assets and is unemployed, he cannot be convicted of the crime of non-support of a child.
       2. The term "sufficient ability" has been held to mean sufficient financial ability.
       3. It does not matter if his unemployment is by choice or unavoidable circumstances.
       4. If he fails to take any steps at all, he may be liable to prosecution for endangering the welfare of a child.
       5. Under the penal law, a parent is responsible for the support of his minor child only if the parent is "of sufficient ability."
       6. An indigent parent may meet his obligation by borrowing money or by seeking aid under the provisions of the Social Welfare Law.

The CORRECT answer is:

  A. 6, 1, 5, 3, 2, 4   B. 1, 3, 5, 2, 4, 6   C. 5, 2, 1, 3, 6, 4
  D. 1, 6, 4, 5, 2, 3

2.____

3. 1. Consider, for example, the case of a rabble rouser who urges a group of twenty people to go out and break the windows of a nearby factory.
    2. Therefore, the law fills the indicated gap with the crime of inciting to riot."
    3. A person is considered guilty of inciting to riot when he urges ten or more persons to engage in tumultuous and violent conduct of a kind likely to create public alarm.
    4. However, if he has not obtained the cooperation of at least four people, he cannot be charged with unlawful assembly.
    5. The charge of inciting to riot was added to the law to cover types of conduct which cannot be classified as either the crime of "riot" or the crime of "unlawful assembly."
    6. If he acquires the acquiescence of at least four of them, he is guilty of unlawful assembly even if the project does not materialize.

    The CORRECT answer is:

    A. 3, 5, 1, 6, 4, 2   B. 5, 1, 4, 6, 2, 3   C. 3, 4, 1, 5, 2, 6
    D. 5, 1, 4, 6, 3, 2

3.____

4. 1. If, however, the rebuttal evidence presents an issue of credibility, it is for the jury to determine whether the presumption has, in fact, been destroyed.
    2. Once sufficient evidence to the contrary is introduced, the presumption disappears from the trial.
    3. The effect of a presumption is to place the burden upon the adversary to come forward with evidence to rebut the presumption.
    4. When a presumption is overcome and ceases to exist in the case, the fact or facts which gave rise to the presumption still remain.
    5. Whether a presumption has been overcome is ordinarily a question for the court.
    6. Such information may furnish a basis for a logical inference.

    The CORRECT answer is:

    A. 4, 6, 2, 5, 1, 3   B. 3, 2, 5, 1, 4, 6   C. 5, 3, 6, 4, 2, 1
    D. 5, 4, 1, 2, 6, 3

4.____

KEY (CORRECT ANSWERS)

1. D
2. C
3. A
4. B

PREPARING WRITTEN MATERIAL

EXAMINATION SECTION
TEST 1

DIRECTIONS: Each of the sentences in the Tests that follow may be classified under one of the following four categories:

    A. *Faulty* because of incorrect grammar or word usage
    B. *Faulty* because of incorrect punctuation
    C. *Faulty* because of incorrect capitalization or incorrect spelling
    D. *Correct*

Examine each sentence carefully to determine under which of the above four options it is best classified. Then, in the space to the right, print the capital letter preceding the option which is the best of the four suggested above.

(Note that each faulty sentence contains but one type of error. Consider a sentence to be correct if it contains none of the types of errors mentioned, even though there may be other correct ways of expressing the same thought.)

1. He sent the notice to the clerk who you hired yesterday.   1._____

2. It must be admitted, however that you were not informed of this change.   2._____

3. Only the employees who have served in this grade for at least two years are eligible for promotion.   3._____

4. The work was divided equally between she and Mary.   4._____

5. He thought that you were not available at that time.   5._____

6. When the messenger returns; please give him this package.   6._____

7. The new secretary prepared, typed, addressed, and delivered, the notices.   7._____

8. Walking into the room, his desk can be seen at the rear.   8._____

9. Although John has worked here longer than She, he produces a smaller amount of work.   9._____

10. She said she could of typed this report yesterday.   10._____

11. Neither one of these procedures are adequate for the efficient performance of this task.   11._____

12. The typewriter is the tool of the typist; the cash register, the tool of the cashier.   12._____

13. "The assignment must be completed as soon as possible" said the supervisor.   13._____

14. As you know, office handbooks are issued to all new Employees.   14._____

15. Writing a speech is sometimes easier than to deliver it before an audience.   15._____

16. Mr. Brown our accountant, will audit the accounts next week.   16._____

17. Give the assignment to whomever is able to do it most efficiently.   17._____

18. The supervisor expected either your or I to file these reports.   18._____

KEY (CORRECT ANSWERS)

1.	A	10.	A
2.	B	11.	A
3.	D	12.	C
4.	A	13.	B
5.	D	14.	C
6.	B	15.	A
7.	B	16.	B
8.	A	17.	A
9.	C	18.	A

TEST 2

DIRECTIONS: Each of the sentences in the Tests that follow may be classified under one of the following four categories:
  A. *Faulty* because of incorrect grammar or word usage
  B. *Faulty* because of incorrect punctuation
  C. *Faulty* because of incorrect capitalization or incorrect spelling
  D. *Correct*

Examine each sentence carefully to determine under which of the above four options it is best classified. Then, in the space to the right, print the capital letter preceding the option which is the best of the four suggested above.

(Note that each faulty sentence contains but one type of error. Consider a sentence to be correct if it contains none of the types of errors mentioned, even though there may be other correct ways of expressing the same thought.)

1. The fire apparently started in the storeroom, which is usually locked.   1._____

2. On approaching the victim, two bruises were noticed by this officer.   2._____

3. The officer, who was there examined the report with great care.   3._____

4. Each employee in the office had a seperate desk.   4._____

5. All employees including members of the clerical staff, were invited to the lecture.   5._____

6. The suggested Procedure is similar to the one now in use.   6._____

7. No one was more pleased with the new procedure than the chauffeur.   7._____

8. He tried to persaude her to change the procedure.   8._____

9. The total of the expenses charged to petty cash were high.   9._____

10. An understanding between him and I was finally reached.   10._____

KEY (CORRECT ANSWERS)

1. D
2. A
3. B
4. C
5. B

6. C
7. D
8. C
9. A
10. A

TEST 3

DIRECTIONS: Each of the sentences in the Tests that follow may be classified under one of the following four categories:
  A. *Faulty* because of incorrect grammar or word usage
  B. *Faulty* because of incorrect punctuation
  C. *Faulty* because of incorrect capitalization or incorrect spelling
  D. *Correct*

Examine each sentence carefully to determine under which of the above four options it is best classified. Then, in the space to the right, print the capital letter preceding the option which is the best of the four suggested above.

(Note that each faulty sentence contains but one type of error. Consider a sentence to be correct if it contains none of the types of errors mentioned, even though there may be other correct ways of expressing the same thought.)

1. They told both he and I that the prisoner had escaped.   1.____

2. Any superior officer, who, disregards the just complaints of his subordinates, is remiss in the performance of his duty.   2.____

3. Only those members of the national organization who resided in the Middle West attended the conference in Chicago.   3.____

4. We told him to give the investigation assignment to whoever was available.   4.____

5. Please do not disappoint and embarass us by not appearing in court.   5.____

6. Although the officer's speech proved to be entertaining, the topic was not relevent to the main theme of the conference.   6.____

7. In February all new officers attended a training course in which they were learned in their principal duties and the fundamental operating procedures of the department.   7.____

8. I personally seen inmate Jones threaten inmates Smith and Green with bodily harm if they refused to participate in the plot.   8.____

9. To the layman, who on a chance visit to the prison observes everything functioning smoothly, the maintenance of prison discipline may seem to be a relatively easily realizable objective.   9.____

10. The prisoners in cell block fourty were forbidden to sit on the cell cots during the recreation hour.   10.____

KEY (CORRECT ANSWERS)

1.	A	6.	C
2.	B	7.	A
3.	C	8.	A
4.	D	9.	D
5.	C	10.	C

TEST 4

DIRECTIONS: Each of the sentences in the Tests that follow may be classified under one of
the following four categories:
A.   *Faulty* because of incorrect grammar or word usage
B.   *Faulty* because of incorrect punctuation
C.   *Faulty* because of incorrect capitalization or incorrect spelling
D.   *Correct*

Examine each sentence carefully to determine under which of the above four options it is
best classified. Then, in the space to the right, print the capital letter preceding the option
which is the best of the four suggested above.

(Note that each faulty sentence contains but one type of error. Consider a sentence to be
correct if it contains none of the types of errors mentioned, even though there may be other
correct ways of expressing the same thought.)

1.   I cannot encourage you any.   1._____

2.   You always look well in those sort of clothes.   2._____

3.   Shall we go to the park?   3._____

4.   The man whome he introduced was Mr. Carey.   4._____

5.   She saw the letter laying here this morning.   5._____

6.   It should rain before the Afternoon is over.   6._____

7.   They have already went home.   7._____

8.   That Jackson will be elected is evident.   8._____

9.   He does not hardly approve of us.   9._____

10.   It was he, who won the prize.   10._____

————————

KEY (CORRECT ANSWERS)

1.	A	6.	C
2.	A	7.	A
3.	D	8.	D
4.	C	9.	A
5.	A	10.	B

———

TEST 5

DIRECTIONS: Each of the sentences in the Tests that follow may be classified under one of the following four categories:
- A. *Faulty* because of incorrect grammar or word usage
- B. *Faulty* because of incorrect punctuation
- C. *Faulty* because of incorrect capitalization or incorrect spelling
- D. *Correct*

Examine each sentence carefully to determine under which of the above four options it is best classified. Then, in the space to the right, print the capital letter preceding the option which is the best of the four suggested above.

(Note that each faulty sentence contains but one type of error. Consider a sentence to be correct if it contains none of the types of errors mentioned, even though there may be other correct ways of expressing the same thought.)

1.   Shall we go to the park.   1.____

2.   They are, alike, in this particular way.   2.____

3.   They gave the poor man sume food when he knocked on the door.   3.____

4.   I regret the loss caused by the error.   4.____

5.   The students' will have a new teacher.   5.____

6.   They sweared to bring out all the facts.   6.____

7.   He decided to open a branch store on 33rd street.   7.____

8.   His speed is equal and more than that of a racehorse.   8.____

9.   He felt very warm on that Summer day.   9.____

10. He was assisted by his friend, who lives in the next house.   10.____

––––––––––

KEY (CORRECT ANSWERS)

1. B	6. A
2. B	7. C
3. C	8. A
4. D	9. C
5. B	10. D

———

TEST 6

DIRECTIONS: Each of the sentences in the Tests that follow may be classified under one of
the following four categories:
A.   *Faulty* because of incorrect grammar or word usage
B.   *Faulty* because of incorrect punctuation
C.   *Faulty* because of incorrect capitalization or incorrect spelling
D.   *Correct*

Examine each sentence carefully to determine under which of the above four options it is
best classified. Then, in the space to the right, print the capital letter preceding the option
which is the best of the four suggested above.

(Note that each faulty sentence contains but one type of error. Consider a sentence to be
correct if it contains none of the types of errors mentioned, even though there may be other
correct ways of expressing the same thought.)

1.   The climate of New York is colder than California.   1._____

2.   I shall wait for you on the corner.   2._____

3.   Did we see the boy who, we think, is the leader.   3._____

4.   Being a modest person, John seldom talks about his invention.   4._____

5.   The gang is called the smith street boys.   5._____

6.   He seen the man break into the store.   6._____

7.   We expected to lay still there for quite a while.   7._____

8.   He is considered to be the Leader of his organization.   8._____

9.   Although I recieved an invitation, I won't go.   9._____

10. The letter must be here some place.   10._____

———

KEY (CORRECT ANSWERS)

1.	A	6.	A
2.	D	7.	A
3.	B	8.	C
4.	D	9.	C
5.	C	10.	A

———

TEST 7

DIRECTIONS: Each of the sentences in the Tests that follow may be classified under one of the following four categories:
- A. *Faulty* because of incorrect grammar or word usage
- B. *Faulty* because of incorrect punctuation
- C. *Faulty* because of incorrect capitalization or incorrect spelling
- D. *Correct*

Examine each sentence carefully to determine under which of the above four options it is best classified. Then, in the space to the right, print the capital letter preceding the option which is the best of the four suggested above.

(Note that each faulty sentence contains but one type of error. Consider a sentence to be correct if it contains none of the types of errors mentioned, even though there may be other correct ways of expressing the same thought.)

1. I though it to be he.   1.____

2. We expect to remain here for a long time.   2.____

3. The committee was agreed.   3.____

4. Two-thirds of the building are finished.   4.____

5. The water was froze.   5.____

6. Everyone of the salesmen must supply their own car.   6.____

7. Who is the author of Gone With the Wind?   7.____

8. He marched on and declaring that he would never surrender.   8.____

9. Who shall I say called?   9.____

10. Everyone has left but they.   10.____

KEY (CORRECT ANSWERS)

1.	A	6.	A
2.	D	7.	B
3.	D	8.	A
4.	A	9.	D
5.	A	10.	D

———

TEST 8

DIRECTIONS: Each of the sentences in the Tests that follow may be classified under one of
the following four categories:
A. *Faulty* because of incorrect grammar or word usage
B. *Faulty* because of incorrect punctuation
C. *Faulty* because of incorrect capitalization or incorrect spelling
D. *Correct*

Examine each sentence carefully to determine under which of the above four options it is best classified. Then, in the space to the right, print the capital letter preceding the option which is the best of the four suggested above.

(Note that each faulty sentence contains but one type of error. Consider a sentence to be correct if it contains none of the types of errors mentioned, even though there may be other correct ways of expressing the same thought.)

1. Who did we give the order to?   1._____

2. Send your order in immediately.   2._____

3. I believe I paid the Bill.   3._____

4. I have not met but one person.   4._____

5. Why aren't Tom, and Fred, going to the dance?   5._____

6. What reason is there for him not going?   6._____

7. The seige of Malta was a tremendous event.   7._____

8. I was there yesterday I assure you.   8._____

9. Your ukelele is better than mine.   9._____

10. No one was there only Mary.   10._____

KEY (CORRECT ANSWERS)

1.	A		6.	A
2.	D		7.	C
3.	C		8.	B
4.	A		9.	C
5.	B		10.	A

———

TEST 9

DIRECTIONS: In each of the following groups of sentences, one of the four sentences is faulty in grammar, punctuation, or capitalization. Select the incorrect sentence in each case.

1.   A.   If you had stood at home and done your homework, you would not have failed in arithmetic.   1._____
      B.   Her affected manner annoyed every member of the audience.
      C.   How will the new law affect our income taxes?
      D.   The plants were not affected by the long, cold winter, but they succumbed to the drought of summer.

2.   A.   He is one of the most able men who have been in the Senate.   2._____
      B.   It is he who is to blame for the lamentable mistake.
      C.   Haven't you a helpful suggestion to make at this time?
      D.   The money was robbed from the blind man's cup.

3.   A.   The amount of children in this school is steadily increasing.   3._____
      B.   After taking an apple from the table, she went out to play.
      C.   He borrowed a dollar from me.
      D.   I had hoped my brother would arrive before me.

4.   A.   Whom do you think I hear from every week?   4._____
      B.   Who do you think is the right man for the job?
      C.   Who do you think I found in the room?
      D.   He is the man whom we considered a good candidate for the presidency.

5.   A.   Quietly the puppy laid down before the fireplace.   5._____
      B.   You have made your bed; now lie in it.
      C.   I was badly sunburned because I had lain too long in the sun.
      D.   I laid the doll on the bed and left the room.

KEY (CORRECT ANSWERS)

1. A
2. D
3. A
4. C
5. A

———

READING COMPREHENSION
UNDERSTANDING AND INTERPRETING WRITTEN MATERIAL

EXAMINATION SECTION
TEST 1

DIRECTIONS: Each question or incomplete statement is followed by several suggested answers or completions. Select the one that BEST answers the question or completes the statement. *PRINT THE LETTER OF THE CORRECT ANSWER IN THE SPACE AT THE RIGHT.*

Questions 1-5.

DIRECTIONS: Questions 1 through 5 are to be answered SOLELY on the basis of the following paragraph.

In counting the poor, the Social Security Administration has developed two poverty thresholds that <u>designate</u> families as either *poor* or *near poor*. The Administration assumed that the poor would spend the same proportion of income on food as the rest of the population but that, obviously, since their income was smaller, their range of selection would be narrower. In the Low Cost Food Plan, the amount <u>allocated to</u> food from the average expenditure was cut to the minimum that the Agriculture Department said could still provide American families with an adequate diet. This Low Cost Food Plan was used to characterize the *near poor* category, and an even lower Economy Food Plan was used to characterize the *poor* category. The Economy Food Plan was based on $7.00 a person for food each day, assuming that all food would be prepared at home. The Agriculture Department estimates that only about 10 percent of persons spending $7.00 or less for food each day actually were able to get a nutritionally adequate diet.

1. Of the following, the MOST suitable title for the above paragraph would be   1.____
   - A. THE SUPERIORITY OF THE ECONOMY PLAN OVER THE LOW COST PLAN
   - B. THE NEED FOR A NUTRITIONALLY ADEQUATE DIET
   - C. FOOD EXPENDITURES OF THE POOR AND THE NEAR POOR
   - D. DIET IN THE UNITED STATES

2. According to the above paragraph, the Social Security Administration assumed,   2.____
   in setting its poverty levels, that the poor
   - A. spend a smaller proportion of income for food than the average non-poor
   - B. would not eat in restaurants
   - C. as a group includes only those with a nutritionally inadequate diet
   - D. spend more money on food than the near poor

3. According to the above paragraph, it would be CORRECT to state that the   3.____
Low Cost Food Plan
   A. is above the minimum set by the Agriculture Department for a nutritionally adequate diet
   B. gives most people a nutritionally inadequate diet
   C. is lower than the Economy Food Plan
   D. represents the amount spent by the near poor

4. As estimated by the Department of Agriculture, the percentage of people   4.____
spending $7.00 or less a day for food who did NOT get a nutritionally adequate
diet was
   A. 100%   B. 90%   C. 10%   D. 0%

5. As used in the above paragraph, the underlined words allocated to mean   5.____
MOST NEARLY
   A. offered for   B. assigned to
   C. wasted on   D. spent on

Questions 6-11.

DIRECTIONS: Questions 6 through 11 are to be answered SOLELY on the basis of the information given in the paragraph below.

Three years ago, the City introduced a program of reduced transit rates for the elderly. It was hoped that this program would increase the travel of the elderly and help them maintain a greater measure of independence. About 600,000 of the 800,000 eligible residents are currently enrolled in the program. To be eligible, a person must be 65 years of age or older and not employed full-time. Riding for reduced fare is permitted between 10:00 A.M. and 4:00 P.M. and between 7:00 P.M. and Midnight on weekdays, and 24 hours a day on Saturdays, Sundays, and holidays.

In a City university study, based on a sampling of 728 enrollees interviewed, it was learned that 51 percent are able to travel more and 30.8 percent had been able to save enough money to make a noticeable difference in their budgets as a result of the reduced-fare program.

It has been recommended that reduced-fare programs be extended to encourage the use of transit lines in off hours by other groups such as the poor, the very young, housewives, and the physically handicapped. To implement this recommendation, it would be necessary for the Federal government to increase transit subsidies.

6. Which one of the following titles would be the BEST for the above passage?   6.____
   A. A PROGRAM OF REDUCED TRANSIT RATES FOR THE ELDERLY
   B. RECOMMENDATIONS FOR EXTENDING PROGRAMS FOR THE ELDERLY
   C. CITY UNIVERSITY STUDY ON THE RELATIONSHIP OF AGE AND TRAVEL
   D. ELIGIBILITY REQUIREMENTS FOR THE REDUCED RATE PROGRAM

7. Approximately what percentage of the eligible residents is currently enrolled in the reduced-fare program?   7.____
    A. 25%   B. 50%   C. 65%   D. 75%

8. Which one of the following persons is NOT eligible for the reduced-fare program? A   8.____
    A. woman, age 67, employed part-time as a stenographer
    B. handicapped man, age 62
    C. blind man, age 66, employed part-time as a transcribing typist
    D. housewife, age 70

9. At which one of the following times would the reduced-fare NOT be permitted for an eligible elderly person?   9.____
    A. Sunday, 6:00 P.M.   B. Christmas Day, 2:00 A.M.
    C. Tuesday, 9:00 A.M.   D. Thursday, 8:00 P.M.

10. Of the 728 enrollees interviewed in the City university study of the reduced-fare program, it was found that   10.____
    A. the majority traveled more and saved money at the same time
    B. more than half traveled less and, therefore, saved money
    C. about half traveled more and about one-third saved money
    D. the majority saved money but traveled the same rate as before

11. According to the above passage, what would be necessary to extend the reduced-fare program to other groups of people?   11.____
    A. Increasing the eligible age to 68
    B. Reducing the hours when half-fare is permitted
    C. Increasing the fare for other riders
    D. Increasing the transit subsidies by the Federal government

Questions 12-14.

DIRECTIONS: Questions 12 through 14 are to be answered SOLELY on the basis of the following passage.

    Local public welfare agencies, in general, recognize that more time is required for Aid to Dependent Children cases and General Assistance cases than for Old Age Assistance cases, and that the intensive work required in Child Welfare Service cases necessitates special planning with regard to limiting caseloads for workers to prevent their carrying too large a number of cases. A General Assistance case often includes several persons, while Old Age Assistance cases are on an individual basis. Although the average cost of a case per month has continued to increase for all assistance programs, these programs have retained their relative cost positions. The average monthly cost of a case has been lowest for Aid to the Aged, followed, in ascending order, by Aid to the Blind, Aid to Dependent Children, and General Assistance, with the cost per case of the last mentioned program averaging more than four times that for Aid to the Aged. On the other hand, the proportion of Aid to the Aged cases is rising while the percentage of General Assistance cases is declining.

12. Some types of cases require more time or more intensive work than others.   12.____
The one of the following statements which MOST accurately illustrates this
point, according to the above paragraph, is:
   A. Aid to the Blind cases often included several persons and, therefore, are
very time-consuming, while Old Age Assistance cases require intensive
casework
   B. Aid to Dependent Children cases often involve complicated situations
and, therefore, require intensive casework, while Aid to the Blind cases
are extremely time-consuming
   C. Old Age Assistance cases are relatively less time-consuming, while Child
Welfare Service cases entail detailed casework
   D. Old Age Assistance cases are time-consuming, while General Assistance
cases are comparatively simple

13. If a public welfare official were to set up several caseloads, with each caseload   13.____
containing the same total number of cases but with a varying number in each of
the different types of assistance, the caseload which would MOST likely require
the GREATEST expenditure of time would be the one with a majority of
   A. Aid to the Blind cases and Aid to Dependent Children cases
   B. General Assistance cases and Aid to Dependent Children cases
   C. Old Age Assistance cases and Aid to the Blind cases
   D. Old Age Assistance cases and General Assistance cases

14. According to the above paragraph, the one of the following statements which   14.____
is the MOST accurate with regard to the cost of welfare services is that
   A. the average monthly cost for each Aid to Dependent Children case was
higher than for each Aid to the Blind case but lower than for each Aid to
the Aged case
   B. the cost per case for General Assistance has risen four times as fast as
the cost per case for Aid to the Aged
   C. there has been a decrease in the proportion of General Assistance cases,
but the cost per case in this category has increased
   D. more than four times as much money was spent in total for all the cases
in the General Assistance program than for those in the Aid to the Aged
program

Questions 15-17.

DIRECTIONS: Questions 15 through 17 are to be answered SOLELY on the basis of the
following passage.

Aid to dependent children shall be given to a parent or other relative as herein specified for
the benefit of a child or children under sixteen years of age or of a minor or minors between
sixteen and eighteen years of age if in the judgment of the administrative agency: (1) the
granting of an allowance will be in the interest of such child or minor, and (2) the parent or other
relative is a fit person to bring up such child or minor so that his physical, mental, and moral
well-being will be safeguarded, and (3) aid is necessary to enable such parent or other relative
to do so, and (4) such child or minor is a resident of the state on the date of application for aid,
and (5) such minor between sixteen and eighteen years of age is regularly attending school in

accordance with the regulations of the department. An allowance may be granted for the aid of such child or minor who has been deprived of parental support or care by reason of the death, continued absence from the home, or physical or mental incapacity of a parent, and who is living with his father, mother, grandfather, grandmother, brother, sister, stepfather, stepmother, stepbrother, stepsister, uncle, or aunt. In making such allowances, consideration shall be given to the ability of the relative making application and of any other relatives to support and are for or to contribute to the support and care of such child or minor. In making all such allowances, it shall be made certain that the religious faith of the child or minor shall be preserved and protected.

15. The above passage is concerned PRIMARILY with   15.____
    A. the financial ability of persons applying for public assistance
    B. compliance on the part of applicants with the *settlement* provisions of the law
    C. the fitness of parents or other relatives to bring up physically, mentally, or morally delinquent children between the ages of sixteen and eighteen
    D. eligibility for aid to dependent children

16. On the basis of the above passage, the MOST accurate of the following   16.____
    statements is:
    A. Mary Doe, mother of John, age 18, is entitled to aid for her son if he is attending school regularly
    B. Evelyn Stowe, mother of Eleanor, age 13, is not entitled to aid for Eleanor if she uses her home for immoral purposes
    C. Ann Roe, cousin of Helen, age 14, is entitled to aid for Helen if the latter is living with her
    D. Peter Moe, uncle of Henry, age 15, is not entitled to aid for Henry if the latter is living with him

17. The above passage is PROBABLY an excerpt of the   17.____
    A. Administrative Code   B. Social Welfare Law
    C. Federal Security Act   D. City Charter

Questions 18-20.

DIRECTIONS: Questions 18 through 20 are to be answered SOLELY on the basis of the information contained in the following passage.

On the state level, in an effort to obtain better administration and delivery of services in the Medicaid program, the Governor has appointed a committee to advise the State Commissioner of Social Welfare on medical care services. Included on this committee are representatives of the medical, dental, pharmaceutical, nursing, and social work professions, as well as persons representing the fields of mental health, home health agencies, nursing homes, schools of health science, public health and welfare administrations, and the general public. Several of the committee members are physicians in private practice who represent and uphold the interests of the private physicians who care for Medicaid patients.

The committee not only makes recommendations on the standards, quality, and costs of medical services, personnel, and facilities, but also helps identify unmet needs, and assists in long-range planning, evaluation, and utilization of services. It advises, as requested, on administrative and fiscal matters, and also interprets the programs and goals to professional groups.

On the city level, representatives of the county medical societies of the city meet periodically with Medicaid administrators to discuss problems and consider proposals. It is hoped that the county medical societies will assume the responsibility of informing citizens as to where they can receive medical care under Medicaid.

18. Based on information in the above passage, it can be inferred that the group on the advisory committee likely to be LEAST objective in their recommendations would be the representatives of the
    A. public health and welfare administrations
    B. general public
    C. private physicians
    D. schools of health science

18.____

19. The above passage suggests that a problem with the Medicaid program is that
    A. the Mayor has not appointed a committee to work with the City Commissioner of Social Services
    B. many people do not know where they can go to obtain medical care under the program
    C. the county medical societies do not meet often enough with the Medicaid program administrators
    D. citizens do not take the initiative to seek out sources of available medical care under the program

19.____

20. According to the above passage, the Governor's objective in appointing the advisory committee was to
    A. obtain more cooperation from the county medical societies
    B. get the members of the committee to provide medical care services to Medicaid recipients
    C. help improve the Medicaid program in all its aspects, including administration and provision of services
    D. persuade a greater number of private physicians and other health care professionals to accept Medicaid patients

20.____

Questions 21-25.

DIRECTIONS: Questions 21 through 25 are to be answered SOLELY on the basis of the
                 following passage.

Any person who is living in the city and is otherwise eligible may be granted public
assistance whether or not he has state residence. However, since the city does not contribute
to the cost of assistance granted to persons who are without state residence, the cases of all
recipients must be formally identified as to whether or not each member of the household has
state residence.

To acquire state residence, a person must have resided in the state continuously for one
year. Such residence is not lost unless the person is out of the state continuously for a period of
one year or longer. Continuous residence does not include any period during which the
individual is a patient in a hospital, an inmate of a public institution or of an incorporated private
institution, a resident on a military reservation or a minor residing in a boarding home while
under the care of an authorized agency. Receipt of public assistance does not prevent a person
from acquiring state residence. State residence, once acquired, is not lost because of absence
from the state while a person is serving in the United States Armed Forces or the Merchant
Marine; nor does a member of the family of such a person lose state residence while living with
or near that person in these circumstances.

Each person, regardless of age, acquires or loses state residence as an individual. There
is no derivative state residence except for an infant at the time of birth. He is deemed to have
state residence if he is in the custody of both parents and either one of them has state
residence, or if the parent having custody of his has state residence.

21.   According to the above passage, an infant is deemed to have state residence   21.____
      at the time of his birth if
      A. he is born in the state but neither of his parents is a resident
      B. he is in the custody of only one parent, who is not a resident but his other
          parent is a resident
      C. his brother and sister are residents
      D. he is in the custody of both his parents but only one of them is a resident

22.   The Jones family consists of five members. Jack and Mary Jones have lived   22.____
      in New York State continuously for the past eighteen months after having lived
      in Ohio since they were born. Of their three children, one was born ten months
      ago and has been in the custody of his parents since birth. Their second child
      lived in Ohio until six months ago and then moved in with his parents. Their
      third child had never lived in New York until he moved with his parents to New
      York eighteen months ago. However, he entered the Armed Forces one month
      later and has not lived in New York since that time. Based on the above
      passage, how many members of the Jones family are New York State
      residents?
      A. 2   B. 3   C. 4   D. 5

23. Assuming that each of the following individuals has lived continuously in the state for the past year, and has never previously lived in the state, which one of them is a state resident?

    A. Jack Salinas, who has been an inmate in a state correctional facility for six months of the year

    B. Fran Johnson, who has lived on an Army base for the entire year

    C. Arlene Snyder, who married a non-resident during the past year

    D. Gary Phillips, who was a patient in a Veterans Administration Hospital for the entire year

23._____

24. The above passage implies that the reason for determining whether or not a recipient of public assistance is a state resident is that

    A. the cost of assistance for non-residents is not a city responsibility

    B. non-residents living in the city are not eligible for public assistance

    C. recipients of public assistance are barred from acquiring state residence

    D. the city is responsible for the full cost of assistance to recipients who are residents

24._____

25. Assume that the Rollins household in the city consists of six members at the present time – Anne Rollins, her three children, her aunt, and her uncle. Anne Rollins and one of her children moved to the city seven months ago. Neither of them had previously lived in the state. Her other two children have lived in the city continuously for the past two years, as has her aunt. Anne Rollins' uncle had lived in the city continuously for many years until two years ago. He then entered the Armed Forces and has returned to the city within the past month. Based on the above passage, how many members of the Rollins' household are state residents?

    A. 2   B. 3   C. 4   D. 6

25._____

———

KEY (CORRECT ANSWERS)

1.	C		11.	D
2.	B		12.	C
3.	D		13.	B
4.	B		14.	C
5.	B		15.	D
6.	A		16.	B
7.	D		17.	B
8.	B		18.	C
9.	C		19.	B
10.	C		20.	C

21.	D
22.	B
23.	C
24.	A
25.	C

———

TEST 2

DIRECTIONS: Each question or incomplete statement is followed by several suggested answers or completions. Select the one that BEST answers the question or completes the statement. *PRINT THE LETTER OF THE CORRECT ANSWER IN THE SPACE AT THE RIGHT.*

Questions 1-4.

DIRECTIONS: Questions 1 through 4 are to be answered SOLELY on the basis of the following passage.

The loss of control over the use of a drug — called addiction where there is both physical and psychological dependence, and habituation where there is psychological dependence without physical dependence — is, regardless of the particular drug involved, a disease. Both chronic alcoholism and narcotics addiction are usually recognized as diseases.

It is inappropriate to invoke the criminal process against persons who have lost control over the use of dangerous drugs solely because these persons are drug users. Once a person has lost control over his use of drugs, the existence of offenses such as drug use or simple possession will not deter his use. Having lost control, he cannot choose to conform his conduct to the requirements of the law by refraining from use. He is non-deterrable.

Admittedly, there may be times before a person loses control over his use of drugs when he did have a choice of whether to use or not to use, or to stop using. Because of this, punishing him for use or simple possession would not offend the principle that to be punishable conduct must be a result of free choice.

1. Of the following, the MOST suitable title for the above passage is   1.____
   A. DRUG ADDICTION
   B. DRUG ABUSE AND PUNISHMENT
   C. HABITUATION AND THE CRIMINAL PROCESS
   D. PREVENTING DRUG-RELATED CRIME

2. According to the above passage, addiction and habituation are   2.____
   A. identical in meaning because both are diseases related to drug use
   B. identical in meaning because both involve dependence on drugs
   C. similar to the extent that both involve physical dependence on a drug
   D. similar to the extent that both involve psychological dependence on a drug

3. According to the above passage, punishing drug abusers would be justifiable   3.____
   ONLY if their behavior were
   A. elective   B. non-deterrable
   C. chronic   D. dangerous

4. According to the above passage, punishing a person for simple possession   4.____
   of drugs is
   A. appropriate under certain circumstances
   B. inappropriate because the person could not have acted otherwise
   C. necessary for the protection of society
   D. unfair because it penalizes past conduct

Questions 5-8.

DIRECTIONS: Questions 5 through 8 are to be answered SOLELY on the basis of the
following passage.

The usually explanation for drunken behavior is that alcohol, which is a physiological depressant, impairs reasoning and inhibition powers before it depresses the ability to act and to express emotion.

The purely physiological effects of alcohol are very much like of those of fatigue. Individual personality and social and cultural influences apparently greatly determine how these effects are reflected in changed behavior as alcohol is consumed. Therefore, one can assert that alcohol alone does not cause drunken behavior; rather, drunken behavior expresses personal character, cultural traditions, and social circumstances, as they influence a person's reactions to the physiological effects of alcohol on his body.

For some people, and in some circumstances, these personal, cultural, and social factors may readily express themselves as criminal behavior. The most obvious case, of course, is public drunkenness.

The exact relationship between various crimes and various stages of intoxication is not completely known. G.M. Scott believes that the moderate stages of intoxication are the ones usually associated with crime since the latter states of intoxication make performance of crime impossible. Dr. Banay found that many drunks are drawn into crime not only by the need of money to replace wages that drinking prevents them from earning, but also by their increased irritability and pugnacity. He discovered that most of the sex offenses for which offenders are committed to state prisons show a relation between alcohol and the crime and that the average sex case is a clear-cut illustration of the hypothesis that alcohol covers up an underlying condition and that some dormant tendency is either brought to the surface or aggravated by alcohol.

In addition to drunken behavior resulting in criminal acts, it is also connected to several other important social problems. Reference can be made particularly to dependency, unemployment, desertion, divorce, vagrancy, and suicide. For all of these social ills, alcohol acts as the physiological depressing agent which influences one's deviation from normative behavior.

5. Discussions of intoxication customarily state that alcohol   5.____
   A. initially affects the analytic faculty
   B. initially affects the ability to express feelings
   C. reduces the desire for money
   D. stimulates perception of the true nature of one's condition

6. Which one of the following hypotheses would Dr. Banay MOST likely support?   6.____
    A. The casual drinker is LESS likely to commit a crime than the chronic drinker.
    B. An aggressive drunk is LIKELY to have aggressive tendencies when not under the influence of alcohol.
    C. The UNDERLYING cause of most sex offenses is excessive drinking.
    D. There is NO connection between cultural background and drunken behavior.

7. The title BEST suited for the above passage is   7.____
    A. HOW ALCOHOL INFLUENCES POTENTIAL SEXUAL OFFENDERS
    B. STAGES OF INTOXICATION
    C. THE ROLE OF ALCOHOLIC CONSUMPTION IN HUMAN BEHAVIOR
    D. THE RELATIONSHIP BETWEEN ALCOHOL AND EMOTION

8. The writer implies that   8.____
    A. a desire to destroy oneself is a frequent side effect of drinking intoxicating liquors
    B. a person who is drunk may find it easier to kill himself
    C. there is a pattern of drinking behavior in the background of most suicides
    D. there is no relationship between the problems of drinking and suicide

Questions 9-11.

DIRECTIONS: Questions 9 through 11 are to be answered SOLELY on the basis of the following paragraph.

A substantial source of opposition to legalizing heroin is those people who are convinced that this idea is simply another form of social and economic injustice. Instead of getting at the fundamental causes of addiction, they say, the result will be to turn hundreds of young addicts into the living dead.

9. According to the above paragraph, opposition to legalizing heroin is based, in part, on the belief that   9.____
    A. some addicts will become walking dead people
    B. the problem is entirely one of educating individuals
    C. the pushers will simply turn to other criminal activities
    D. the root causes of addiction are still mysterious

10. Which of the following treatment approaches would the author of the above paragraph be MOST likely to oppose?   10.____
    A. Ambulatory detoxification   B. Methadone maintenance
    C. Drug-free therapeutic community   D. Youth intervention program

11. As used in the above paragraph, the underlined word substantial means MOST NEARLY   11.____
    A. known   B. large   C. strange   D. unanimous

Questions 12-16.

DIRECTIONS: Questions 12 through 16 are to be answered SOLELY on the basis of the following paragraph.

In the last dozen years or so, there has <u>emerged</u> an argument which obviously has a certain persuasiveness among young people: that drugs are being used, not as an expression of antisocial behavior or for escape, but to define a different, anti-establishment culture. Drugs can, of course, be used that way; it's very possible to have a youth culture that uses drugs as a <u>norm</u>. But it's also possible to have a youth culture that is opposed to using drugs as a <u>norm</u>. For example, in China, around 1910, a very effective campaign against opium was led largely by students who felt that the use of drugs was the reason China had suffered so much at the hands of the Western powers.

12. According to the above paragraph, the Chinese students opposed the use of opium because   12.____
   A. it contradicted Chinese religious values
   B. it interfered with their studies
   C. they believed it weakened their country
   D. the Western powers encouraged addiction

13. The writer of the above paragraph seems to believe that there is no necessary connection between   13.____
   A. escapism and culture
   B. norms and values
   C. students and politics
   D. youth and drugs

14. According to the above paragraph, it is possible to have a youth culture that considers the use of drugs   14.____
   A. completely acceptable
   B. legally defensible
   C. morally uplifting
   D. physically beneficial

15. The underlined word <u>emerged</u> means MOST NEARLY   15.____
   A. come into view
   B. gone through
   C. required to be
   D. responded quickly

16. As used in the above paragraph, the underlined word <u>norm</u> means MOST NEARLY   16.____
   A. argument of explanation
   B. error or mistake
   C. pleasure or reward
   D. rule or average

Questions 17-20.

DIRECTIONS: Questions 17 through 20 are to be answered SOLELY on the basis of the following paragraph.

Alcoholics are to be found in both sexes, in every major religious and racial group, and at all socio-economic levels. What they share in common are psychiatric problems which they seek to ease or dull through alcohol. Ideally, every heavy drinker should be subjected to intensive psychiatric therapy. Unfortunately, even psychiatric treatment is not always successful, and in any case the nation has allocated neither the funds nor the personnel nor the facilities that would be required for such a massive therapeutic effort.

17. According to the above paragraph, national priorities in connection with   17.____
    psychiatric treatment for alcoholism do NOT provide for
       A. fair and impartial treatment   B. large-scale programs
       C. proper religious values   D. strict laws against alcoholism

18. According to the above paragraph, alcoholics are MOST likely to be   18.____
       A. emotionally disturbed   B. ultimately curable
       C. unable to function   D. under medical care

19. As used in the above paragraph, the underlined word intensive means MOST   19.____
    NEARLY
       A. concentrated   B. modern   C. prompt   D. specialized

20. As used in the above paragraph, the underlined word allocated means   20.____
    MOST NEARLY
       A. assigned   B. conserved   C. desired   D. recognized

Questions 21-25.

DIRECTIONS: Questions 21 through 25 are to be answered SOLELY on the basis of the following paragraph.

The practice of occasionally adulterating marijuana complicates analysis of the effects of marijuana use in non-controlled settings. Behavioral changes which are attributed to marijuana may actually derive from the adulterants or from the interaction of tetrahydrocannabinols and adulterants. Similarly, in today's society, marijuana is often used simultaneously or sequentially with other psycho-active drugs. When drug interactions occur, the simultaneous presence of two or more drugs in the body can exert effects which are more than that which would result from the simple addition of the effects of each drug used separately. Thus, the total behavioral response may be greater than the sum of its parts. For example, if a given dose of marijuana induced two units of perceptual distortion, and a certain dose of LSD given alone induced two units of perceptual distortion, the simultaneous administration of these doses of marijuana and LSD may induce not four but five units of perceptual distortion.

21. According to the above paragraph, the concurrent presence of two drugs in   21.____
the body can
     A. compound the effects of both drugs
     B. reduce perceptual distortion
     C. simulate psychotic symptoms
     D. be highly toxic

22. Based on the above paragraph, it is MOST reasonable to assume that   22.____
tetrahydrocannabinols are
     A. habit-forming substances   B. components of marijuana
     C. similar to quinine or milk-sugar   D. used as adulterants

23. Based on the above paragraph, it is MOSTS reasonable to state that   23.____
marijuana is
     A. most affected by adulterants when used as a psycho-active drug
     B. erroneously considered to be less harmful than other drugs
     C. frequently used in connection with other mind-affecting drugs
     D. occasionally used as an adjunct to LSD in order to reduce bad reactions

24. As used in the above paragraph, the underlined word attributed means   24.____
MOST NEARLY
     A. originally unsuspected   B. identical in action
     C. known as a reason   D. ascribed by way of cause

25. As used in the above paragraph, the underlined word induced means MOST   25.____
NEARLY
     A. caused   B. projected   C. required   D. displayed

————

KEY (CORRECT ANSWERS)

1.	B		11.	B
2.	D		12.	C
3.	A		13.	D
4.	A		14.	A
5.	A		15.	A
6.	B		16.	D
7.	C		17.	B
8.	B		18.	A
9.	A		19.	A
10.	B		20.	A

21.	A
22.	B
23.	C
24.	D
25.	A

PHILOSOPHY, PRINCIPLES, PRACTICES AND TECHNICS
OF
SUPERVISION, ADMINISTRATION, MANAGEMENT AND ORGANIZATION

TABLE OF CONTENTS

Page

I.   MEANING OF SUPERVISION   1

II. THE OLD AND THE NEW SUPERVISION   1

III. THE EIGHT (8) BASIC PRINCIPLES OF THE NEW
     SUPERVISION   1
     1. Principle of Responsibility   1
     2. Principle of Authority   2
     3. Principle of Self-Growth   2
     4. Principle of Individual Worth   2
     5. Principle of Creative Leadership   2
     6. Principle of Success and Failure   2
     7. Principle of Science   3
     8. Principle of Cooperation   3

IV. WHAT IS ADMINISTRATION?   3
     1. Practices commonly classed as "Supervisory"   3
     2. Practices commonly classed as "Administrative"   3
     3. Practices classified as both "Supervisory" and "Administrative"   4

V.   RESPONSIBILITIES OF THE SUPERVISOR   4

VI. COMPETENCIES OF THE SUPERVISOR   4

VII. THE PROFESSIONAL SUPERVISOR—EMPLOYEE RELATIONSHIP   4

VIII. MINI-TEXT IN SUPERVISION, ADMINISTRATION, MANAGEMENT
     AND ORGANIZATION   5
     A. Brief Highlights   5
        1. Levels of Management   5
        2. What the Supervisor Must Learn   6
        3. A Definition of Supervision   6
        4. Elements of the Team Concept   6
        5. Principles of Organization   6
        6. The Four Important Parts of Every Job   6
        7. Principles of Delegation   6
        8. Principles of Effective Communications   7
        9. Principles of Work Improvement   7

TABLE OF CONTENTS (CONTINUED)

10. Areas of Job Improvement 7
11. Seven Key Points in Making Improvements 7
12. Corrective Techniques for Job Improvement 7
13. A Planning Checklist 8
14. Five Characteristics of Good Directions 8
15. Types of Directions 8
16. Controls 8
17. Orienting the New Employee 8
18. Checklist for Orienting New Employees 8
19. Principles of Learning 9
20. Causes of Poor Performance 9
21. Four Major Steps in On-The-Job Instructions 9
22. Employees Want Five Things 9
23. Some Don'ts in Regard to Praise 9
24. How to Gain Your Workers' Confidence 9
25. Sources of Employee Problems 9
26. The Supervisor's Key to Discipline 10
27. Five Important Processes of Management 10
28. When the Supervisor Fails to Plan 10
29. Fourteen General Principles of Management 10
30. Change 10

B. Brief Topical Summaries 11
    I.   Who/What is the Supervisor? 11
    II.   The Sociology of Work 11
    III.   Principles and Practices of Supervision 12
    IV.   Dynamic Leadership 12
    V.   Processes for Solving Problems 12
    VI.   Training for Results 13
    VII.   Health, Safety and Accident Prevention 13
    VIII.   Equal Employment Opportunity 13
    IX.   Improving Communications 14
    X.   Self-Development 14
    XI.   Teaching and Training 14
            A. The Teaching Process 14
                1. Preparation 14
                2. Presentation 15
                3. Summary 15
                4. Application 15
                5. Evaluation 15
            B. Teaching Methods 15
                1. Lecture 15
                2. Discussion 15
                3. Demonstration 16
                4. Performance 16
                5. Which Method to Use 16

PHILOSOPHY, PRINCIPLES, PRACTICES, AND TECHNICS
OF
SUPERVISION, ADMINISTRATION, MANAGEMENT AND ORGANIZATION

I. MEANING OF SUPERVISION

The extension of the democratic philosophy has been accompanied by an extension in the scope of supervision. Modern leaders and supervisors no longer think of supervision in the narrow sense of being confined chiefly to visiting employees, supplying materials, or rating the staff. They regard supervision as being intimately related to all the concerned agencies of society, they speak of the supervisor's function in terms of "growth", rather than the "improvement," of employees.

This modern concept of supervision may be defined as follows:

Supervision is leadership and the development of leadership within groups which are cooperatively engaged in inspection, research, training, guidance and evaluation.

II. THE OLD AND THE NEW SUPERVISION

TRADITIONAL
1. Inspection
2. Focused on the employee
3. Visitation
4. Random and haphazard
5. Imposed and authoritarian
6. One person usually

MODERN
1. Study and analysis
2. Focused on aims, materials, methods, supervisors, employees, environment
3. Demonstrations, intervisitation, workshops, directed reading, bulletins, etc.
4. Definitely organized and planned (scientific)
5. Cooperative and democratic
6. Many persons involved (creative)

III THE EIGHT (8) BASIC PRINCIPLES OF THE NEW SUPERVISION

1. *PRINCIPLE OF RESPONSIBILITY*
Authority to act and responsibility for acting must be joined.
   a. If you give responsibility, give authority.
   b. Define employee duties clearly.
   c. Protect employees from criticism by others.
   d. Recognize the rights as well as obligations of employees.
   e. Achieve the aims of a democratic society insofar as it is possible within the area of your work.
   f. Establish a situation favorable to training and learning.
   g. Accept ultimate responsibility for everything done in your section, unit, office, division, department.
   h. Good administration and good supervision are inseparable.

2. *PRINCIPLE OF AUTHORITY*
The success of the supervisor is measured by the extent to which the power of authority is not used.
    a. Exercise simplicity and informality in supervision.
    b. Use the simplest machinery of supervision.
    c. If it is good for the organization as a whole, it is probably justified.
    d. Seldom be arbitrary or authoritative.
    e. Do not base your work on the power of position or of personality.
    f. Permit and encourage the free expression of opinions.

3. *PRINCIPLE OF SELF-GROWTH*
The success of the supervisor is measured by the extent to which, and the speed with which, he is no longer needed.
    a. Base criticism on principles, not on specifics.
    b. Point out higher activities to employees.
    c. Train for self-thinking by employees, to meet new situations.
    d. Stimulate initiative, self-reliance and individual responsibility.
    e. Concentrate on stimulating the growth of employees rather than on removing defects.

4. *PRINCIPLE OF INDIVIDUAL WORTH*
Respect for the individual is a paramount consideration in supervision.
    a. Be human and sympathetic in dealing with employees.
    b. Don't nag about things to be done.
    c. Recognize the individual differences among employees and seek opportunities to permit best expression of each personality.

5. *PRINCIPLE OF CREATIVE LEADERSHIP*
The best supervision is that which is not apparent to the employee.
    a. Stimulate, don't drive employees to creative action.
    b. Emphasize doing good things.
    c. Encourage employees to do what they do best.
    d. Do not be too greatly concerned with details of subject or method.
    e. Do not be concerned exclusively with immediate problems and activities.
    f. Reveal higher activities and make them both desired and maximally possible.
    g. Determine procedures in the light of each situation but see that these are derived from a sound basic philosophy.
    h. Aid, inspire and lead so as to liberate the creative spirit latent in all good employees.

6. *PRINCIPLE OF SUCCESS AND FAILURE*
There are no unsuccessful employees, only unsuccessful supervisors who have failed to give proper leadership.
    a. Adapt suggestions to the capacities, attitudes, and prejudices of employees.
    b. Be gradual, be progressive, be persistent.
    c. Help the employee find the general principle; have the employee apply his own problem to the general principle.
    d. Give adequate appreciation for good work and honest effort.
    e. Anticipate employee difficulties and help to prevent them.
    f. Encourage employees to do the desirable things they will do anyway.
    g. Judge your supervision by the results it secures.

7. *PRINCIPLE OF SCIENCE*
Successful supervision is scientific, objective, and experimental. It is based on facts, not on prejudices.
    a. Be cumulative in results.
    b. Never divorce your suggestions from the goals of training.
    c. Don't be impatient of results.
    d. Keep all matters on a professional, not a personal level.
    e. Do not be concerned exclusively with immediate problems and activities.
    f. Use objective means of determining achievement and rating where possible.

8. *PRINCIPLE OF COOPERATION*
Supervision is a cooperative enterprise between supervisor and employee.
    a. Begin with conditions as they are.
    b. Ask opinions of all involved when formulating policies.
    c. Organization is as good as its weakest link.
    d. Let employees help to determine policies and department programs.
    e. Be approachable and accessible - physically and mentally.
    f. Develop pleasant social relationships.

IV. WHAT IS ADMINISTRATION?

Administration is concerned with providing the environment, the material facilities, and the operational procedures that will promote the maximum growth and development of supervisors and employees. (Organization is an aspect, and a concomitant, of administration.)

There is no sharp line of demarcation between supervision and administration; these functions are intimately interrelated and, often, overlapping. They are complementary activities.

1. *PRACTICES COMMONLY CLASSED AS "SUPERVISORY"*
    a. Conducting employees conferences
    b. Visiting sections, units, offices, divisions, departments
    c. Arranging for demonstrations
    d. Examining plans
    e. Suggesting professional reading
    f. Interpreting bulletins
    g. Recommending in-service training courses
    h. Encouraging experimentation
    i. Appraising employee morale
    j. Providing for intervisitation

2. *PRACTICES COMMONLY CLASSIFIED AS "ADMINISTRATIVE"*
    a. Management of the office
    b. Arrangement of schedules for extra duties
    c. Assignment of rooms or areas
    d. Distribution of supplies
    e. Keeping records and reports
    f. Care of audio-visual materials
    g. Keeping inventory records
    h. Checking record cards and books
    i. Programming special activities
    j. Checking on the attendance and punctuality of employees

3. *PRACTICES COMMONLY CLASSIFIED AS BOTH "SUPERVISORY" AND "ADMINISTRATIVE"*
   - a. Program construction
   - b. Testing or evaluating outcomes
   - c. Personnel accounting
   - d. Ordering instructional materials

V. RESPONSIBILITIES OF THE SUPERVISOR

A person employed in a supervisory capacity must constantly be able to improve his own efficiency and ability. He represents the employer to the employees and only continuous self-examination can make him a capable supervisor.

Leadership and training are the supervisor's responsibility. An efficient working unit is one in which the employees work with the supervisor. It is his job to bring out the best in his employees. He must always be relaxed, courteous and calm in his association with his employees. Their feelings are important, and a harsh attitude does not develop the most efficient employees.

VI. COMPETENCIES OF THE SUPERVISOR

1. Complete knowledge of the duties and responsibilities of his position.
2. To be able to organize a job, plan ahead and carry through.
3. To have self-confidence and initiative.
4. To be able to handle the unexpected situation and make quick decisions.
5. To be able to properly train subordinates in the positions they are best suited for.
6. To be able to keep good human relations among his subordinates.
7. To be able to keep good human relations between his subordinates and himself and to earn their respect and trust.

VII. THE PROFESSIONAL SUPERVISOR-EMPLOYEE RELATIONSHIP

There are two kinds of efficiency: one kind is only apparent and is produced in organizations through the exercise of mere discipline; this is but a simulation of the second, or true, efficiency which springs from spontaneous cooperation. If you are a manager, no matter how great or small your responsibility, it is your job, in the final analysis, to create and develop this involuntary cooperation among the people whom you supervise. For, no matter how powerful a combination of money, machines, and materials a company may have, this is a dead and sterile thing without a team of willing, thinking and articulate people to guide it.

The following 21 points are presented as indicative of the exemplary basic relationship that should exist between supervisor and employee:

1. Each person wants to be liked and respected by his fellow employee and wants to be treated with consideration and respect by his superior.
2. The most competent employee will make an error. However, in a unit where good relations exist between the supervisor and his employees, tenseness and fear do not exist. Thus, errors are not hidden or covered up and the efficiency of a unit is not impaired.
3. Subordinates resent rules, regulations, or orders that are unreasonable or unexplained.
4. Subordinates are quick to resent unfairness, harshness, injustices and favoritism.
5. An employee will accept responsibility if he knows that he will be complimented for a job well done, and not too harshly chastised for failure; that his supervisor will check the cause of the failure, and, if it was the supervisor's fault, he will assume the blame therefore. If it was the employee's fault, his supervisor will explain the correct method or means of handling the responsibility.

6. An employee wants to receive credit for a suggestion he has made, that is used. If a suggestion cannot be used, the employee is entitled to an explanation. The supervisor should not say "no" and close the subject.
7. Fear and worry slow up a worker's ability. Poor working environment can impair his physical and mental health. A good supervisor avoids forceful methods, threats and arguments to get a job done.
8. A forceful supervisor is able to train his employees individually and as a team, and is able to motivate them in the proper channels.
9. A mature supervisor is able to properly evaluate his subordinates and to keep them happy and satisfied.
10. A sensitive supervisor will never patronize his subordinates.
11. A worthy supervisor will respect his employees' confidences.
12. Definite and clear-cut responsibilities should be assigned to each executive.
13. Responsibility should always be coupled with corresponding authority.
14. No change should be made in the scope or responsibilities of a position without a definite understanding to that effect on the part of all persons concerned.
15. No executive or employee, occupying a single position in the organization, should be subject to definite orders from more than one source.
16. Orders should never be given to subordinates over the head of a responsible executive. Rather than do this, the officer in question should be supplanted.
17. Criticisms of subordinates should, whoever possible, be made privately, and in no case should a subordinate be criticized in the presence of executives or employees of equal or lower rank.
18. No dispute or difference between executives or employees as to authority or responsibilities should be considered too trivial for prompt and careful adjudication.
19. Promotions, wage changes, and disciplinary action should always be approved by the executive immediately superior to the one directly responsible.
20. No executive or employee should ever be required, or expected, to be at the same time an assistant to, and critic of, another.
21. Any executive whose work is subject to regular inspection should, whever practicable, be given the assistance and facilities necessary to enable him to maintain an independent check of the quality of his work.

VIII. MINI-TEXT IN SUPERVISION, ADMINISTRATION, MANAGEMENT, AND ORGANIZATION

A. BRIEF HIGHLIGHTS

Listed concisely and sequentially are major headings and important data in the field for quick recall and review.

1. *LEVELS OF MANAGEMENT*
   Any organization of some size has several levels of management. In terms of a ladder the levels are:

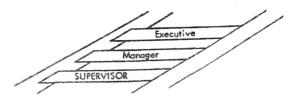

The first level is very important because it is the beginning point of management leadership.

2. *WHAT THE SUPERVISOR MUST LEARN*
   A supervisor must learn to:
   (1) Deal with people and their differences
   (2) Get the job done through people
   (3) Recognize the problems when they exist
   (4) Overcome obstacles to good performance
   (5) Evaluate the performance of people
   (6) Check his own performance in terms of accomplishment

3. *A DEFINITION OF SUPERVISOR*
   The term supervisor means any individual having authority, in the interests of the employer, to hire, transfer, suspend, lay-off, recall, promote, discharge, assign, reward, or discipline other employees or responsibility to direct them, or to adjust their grievances, or effectively to recommend such action, if, in connection with the foregoing, exercise of such authority is not of a merely routine or clerical nature but requires the use of independent judgment.

4. *ELEMENTS OF THE TEAM CONCEPT*
   What is involved in teamwork? The component parts are:
(1) Members	(3) Goals	(5) Cooperation
(2) A leader	(4) Plans	(6) Spirit

5. *PRINCIPLES OF ORGANIZATION*
   (1) A team member must know what his job is.
   (2) Be sure that the nature and scope of a job are understood.
   (3) Authority and responsibility should be carefully spelled out.
   (4) A supervisor should be permitted to make the maximum number of decisions affecting his employees.
   (5) Employees should report to only one supervisor.
   (6) A supervisor should direct only as many employees as he can handle effectively.
   (7) An organization plan should be flexible.
   (8) Inspection and performance of work should be separate.
   (9) Organizational problems should receive immediate attention.
   (10) Assign work in line with ability and experience.

6. *THE FOUR IMPORTANT PARTS OF EVERY JOB*
   (1) Inherent in every job is the *accountability* for results.
   (2) A second set of factors in every job is *responsibilities*.
   (3) Along with duties and responsibilities one must have the *authority* to act within certain limits without obtaining permission to proceed.
   (4) No job exists in a vacuum. The supervisor is surrounded by key *relationships*.

7. *PRINCIPLES OF DELEGATION*
   Where work is delegated for the first time, the supervisor should think in terms of these questions:
   (1) Who is best qualified to do this?
   (2) Can an employee improve his abilities by doing this?
   (3) How long should an employee spend on this?
   (4) Are there any special problems for which he will need guidance?
   (5) How broad a delegation can I make?

8. PRINCIPLES OF EFFECTIVE COMMUNICATIONS
(1) Determine the media
(2) To whom directed?
(3) Identification and source authority
(4) Is communication understood?

9. PRINCIPLES OF WORK IMPROVEMENT
(1) Most people usually do only the work which is assigned to them
(2) Workers are likely to fit assigned work into the time available to perform it
(3) A good workload usually stimulates output
(4) People usually do their best work when they know that results will be reviewed or inspected
(5) Employees usually feel that someone else is responsible for conditions of work, workplace layout, job methods, type of tools/equipment, and other such factors
(6) Employees are usually defensive about their job security
(7) Employees have natural resistance to change
(8) Employees can support or destroy a supervisor
(9) A supervisor usually earns the respect of his people through his personal example of diligence and efficiency

10. AREAS OF JOB IMPROVEMENT
The areas of job improvement are quite numerous, but the most common ones which a supervisor can identify and utilize are:

(1) Departmental layout
(2) Flow of work
(3) Workplace layout
(4) Utilization of manpower
(5) Work methods
(6) Materials handling
(7) Utilization
(8) Motion economy

11. SEVEN KEY POINTS IN MAKING IMPROVEMENTS
(1) Select the job to be improved
(2) Study how it is being done now
(3) Question the present method
(4) Determine actions to be taken
(5) Chart proposed method
(6) Get approval and apply
(7) Solicit worker participation

12. CORRECTIVE TECHNIQUES OF JOB IMPROVEMENT

Specific Problems	General Improvement	Corrective Techniques
(1) Size of workload	(1) Departmental layout	(1) Study with scale model
(2) Inability to meet schedules	(2) Flow of work	(2) Flow chart study
(3) Strain and fatigue	(3) Work plan layout	(3) Motion analysis
(4) Improper use of men and skills	(4) Utilization of manpower	(4) Comparison of units produced to standard allowance
(5) Waste, poor quality, unsafe conditions	(5) Work methods	(5) Methods analysis
(6) Bottleneck conditions that hinder output	(6) Materials handling	(6) Flow chart & equipment study
(7) Poor utilization of equipment and machine	(7) Utilization of equipment	(7) Down time vs. running time
(8) Efficiency and productivity of labor	(8) Motion economy	(8) Motion analysis

13. *A PLANNING CHECKLIST*
(1) Objectives   (6) Resources   (11) Safety
(2) Controls   (7) Manpower   (12) Money
(3) Delegations   (8) Equipment   (13) Work
(4) Communications   (9) Supplies and materials   (14) Timing of improvements
(5) Resources   (10) Utilization of time

14. *FIVE CHARACTERISTICS OF GOOD DIRECTIONS*
In order to get results, directions must be:
(1) Possible of accomplishment   (3) Related to mission   (5) Unmistakably clear
(2) Agreeable with worker interests   (4) Planned and complete

15. *TYPES OF DIRECTIONS*
(1) Demands or direct orders   (3) Suggestion or implication
(2) Requests   (4) Volunteering

16. *CONTROLS*
A typical listing of the overall areas in which the supervisor should establish controls might be:
(1) Manpower   (3) Quality of work   (5) Time   (7) Money
(2) Materials   (4) Quantity of work   (6) Space   (8) Methods

17. *ORIENTING THE NEW EMPLOYEE*
(1) Prepare for him   (3) Orientation for the job
(2) Welcome the new employee   (4) Follow-up

18. *CHECKLIST FOR ORIENTING NEW EMPLOYEES*   Yes No
(1) Do your appreciate the feelings of new employees when they first report for work?
(2) Are you aware of the fact that the new employee must make a big adjustment to his job?
(3) Have you given him good reasons for liking the job and the organization?
(4) Have you prepared for his first day on the job?
(5) Did you welcome him cordially and make him feel needed?
(6) Did you establish rapport with him so that he feels free to talk and discuss matters with you?
(7) Did you explain his job to him and his relationship to you?
(8) Does he know that his work will be evaluated periodically on a basis that is fair and objective?
(9) Did you introduce him to his fellow workers in such a way that they are likely to accept him?
(10) Does he know what employee benefits he will receive?
(11) Does he understand the importance of being on the job and what to do if he must leave his duty station?
(12) Has he been impressed with the importance of accident prevention and safe practice?
(13) Does he generally know his way around the department?
(14) Is he under the guidance of a sponsor who will teach the right ways of doing things?
(15) Do you plan to follow-up so that he will continue to adjust successfully to his job?

19. *PRINCIPLES OF LEARNING*
    (1) Motivation   (2) Demonstration or explanation   (3) Practice

20. *CAUSES OF POOR PERFORMANCE*
    (1) Improper training for job
    (2) Wrong tools
    (3) Inadequate directions
    (4) Lack of supervisory follow-up
    (5) Poor communications
    (6) Lack of standards of performance
    (7) Wrong work habits
    (8) Low morale
    (9) Other

21. *FOUR MAJOR STEPS IN ON-THE-JOB INSTRUCTION*
    (1) Prepare the worker
    (2) Present the operation
    (3) Tryout performance
    (4) Follow-up

22. *EMPLOYEES WANT FIVE THINGS*
    (1) Security (2) Opportunity (3) Recognition (4) Inclusion (5) Expression

23. *SOME DON'TS IN REGARD TO PRAISE*
    (1) Don't praise a person for something he hasn't done
    (2) Don't praise a person unless you can be sincere
    (3) Don't be sparing in praise just because your superior withholds it from you
    (4) Don't let too much time elapse between good performance and recognition of it

24. *HOW TO GAIN YOUR WORKERS' CONFIDENCE*
Methods of developing confidence include such things as:
    (1) Knowing the interests, habits, hobbies of employees
    (2) Admitting your own inadequacies
    (3) Sharing and telling of confidence in others
    (4) Supporting people when they are in trouble
    (5) Delegating matters that can be well handled
    (6) Being frank and straightforward about problems and working conditions
    (7) Encouraging others to bring their problems to you
    (8) Taking action on problems which impede worker progress

25. *SOURCES OF EMPLOYEE PROBLEMS*
On-the-job causes might be such things as:
    (1) A feeling that favoritism is exercised in assignments
    (2) Assignment of overtime
    (3) An undue amount of supervision
    (4) Changing methods or systems
    (5) Stealing of ideas or trade secrets
    (6) Lack of interest in job
    (7) Threat of reduction in force
    (8) Ignorance or lack of communications
    (9) Poor equipment
  (10) Lack of knowing how supervisor feels toward employee
  (11) Shift assignments

Off-the-job problems might have to do with:
    (1) Health   (2) Finances   (3) Housing   (4) Family

26. THE SUPERVISOR'S KEY TO DISCIPLINE
There are several key points about discipline which the supervisor should keep in mind:
- (1) Job discipline is one of the disciplines of life and is directed by the supervisor.
- (2) It is more important to correct an employee fault than to fix blame for it.
- (3) Employee performance is affected by problems both on the job and off.
- (4) Sudden or abrupt changes in behavior can be indications of important employee problems.
- (5) Problems should be dealt with as soon as possible after they are identified.
- (6) The attitude of the supervisor may have more to do with solving problems than the techniques of problem solving.
- (7) Correction of employee behavior should be resorted to only after the supervisor is sure that training or counseling will not be helpful.
- (8) Be sure to document your disciplinary actions.
- (9) Make sure that you are disciplining on the basis of facts rather than personal feelings.
- (10) Take each disciplinary step in order, being careful not to make snap judgments, or decisions based on impatience.

27. FIVE IMPORTANT PROCESSES OF MANAGEMENT
- (1) Planning
- (2) Organizing
- (3) Scheduling
- (4) Controlling
- (5) Motivating

28. WHEN THE SUPERVISOR FAILS TO PLAN
- (1) Supervisor creates impression of not knowing his job
- (2) May lead to excessive overtime
- (3) Job runs itself -- supervisor lacks control
- (4) Deadlines and appointments missed
- (5) Parts of the work go undone
- (6) Work interrupted by emergencies
- (7) Sets a bad example
- (8) Uneven workload creates peaks and valleys
- (9) Too much time on minor details at expense of more important tasks

29. FOURTEEN GENERAL PRINCIPLES OF MANAGEMENT
- (1) Division of work
- (2) Authority and responsibility
- (3) Discipline
- (4) Unity of command
- (5) Unity of direction
- (6) Subordination of individual interest to general interest
- (7) Remuneration of personnel
- (8) Centralization
- (9) Scalar chain
- (10) Order
- (11) Equity
- (12) Stability of tenure of personnel
- (13) Initiative
- (14) Esprit de corps

30. CHANGE
Bringing about change is perhaps attempted more often, and yet less well understood, than anything else the supervisor does. How do people generally react to change? (People tend to resist change that is imposed upon them by other individuals or circumstances.

Change is characteristic of every situation. It is a part of every real endeavor where the efforts of people are concerned.

A. Why do people resist change?
    People may resist change because of:
        (1) Fear of the unknown
        (2) Implied criticism
        (3) Unpleasant experiences in the past
        (4) Fear of loss of status
        (5) Threat to the ego
        (6) Fear of loss of economic stability

B. How can we best overcome the resistance to change?
    In initiating change, take these steps:
        (1) Get ready to sell
        (2) Identify sources of help
        (3) Anticipate objections
        (4) Sell benefits
        (5) Listen in depth
        (6) Follow up

B. BRIEF TOPICAL SUMMARIES

I. WHO/WHAT IS THE SUPERVISOR?

1. The supervisor is often called the "highest level employee and the lowest level manager."
2. A supervisor is a member of both management and the work group. He acts as a bridge between the two.
3. Most problems in supervision are in the area of human relations, or people problems.
4. Employees expect: Respect, opportunity to learn and to advance, and a sense of belonging, and so forth.
5. Supervisors are responsible for directing people and organizing work. Planning is of paramount importance.
6. A position description is a set of duties and responsibilities inherent to a given position.
7. It is important to keep the position description up-to-date and to provide each employee with his own copy.

II. THE SOCIOLOGY OF WORK

1. People are alike in many ways; however, each individual is unique.
2. The supervisor is challenged in getting to know employee differences. Acquiring skills in evaluating individuals is an asset.
3. Maintaining meaningful working relationships in the organization is of great importance.
4. The supervisor has an obligation to help individuals to develop to their fullest potential.
5. Job rotation on a planned basis helps to build versatility and to maintain interest and enthusiasm in work groups.
6. Cross training (job rotation) provides backup skills.
7. The supervisor can help reduce tension by maintaining a sense of humor, providing guidance to employees, and by making reasonable and timely decisions. Employees respond favorably to working under reasonably predictable circumstances.
8. Change is characteristic of all managerial behavior. The supervisor must adjust to changes in procedures, new methods, technological changes, and to a number of new and sometimes challenging situations.
9. To overcome the natural tendency for people to resist change, the supervisor should become more skillful in initiating change.

III. PRINCIPLES AND PRACTICES OF SUPERVISION

    1. Employees should be required to answer to only one superior.

    2. A supervisor can effectively direct only a limited number of employees, depending upon the complexity, variety, and proximity of the jobs involved.

    3. The organizational chart presents the organization in graphic form. It reflects lines of authority and responsibility as well as interrelationships of units within the organization.

    4. Distribution of work can be improved through an analysis using the "Work Distribution Chart."

    5. The "Work Distribution Chart" reflects the division of work within a unit in understandable form.

    6. When related tasks are given to an employee, he has a better chance of increasing his skills through training.

    7. The individual who is given the responsibility for tasks must also be given the appropriate authority to insure adequate results.

    8. The supervisor should delegate repetitive, routine work. Preparation of recurring reports, maintaining leave and attendance records are some examples.

    9. Good discipline is essential to good task performance. Discipline is reflected in the actions of employees on the job in the absence of supervision.

    10. Disciplinary action may have to be taken when the positive aspects of discipline have failed. Reprimand, warning, and suspension are examples of disciplinary action.

    11. If a situation calls for a reprimand, be sure it is deserved and remember it is to be done in private.

IV. DYNAMIC LEADERSHIP

    1. A style is a personal method or manner of exerting influence.

    2. Authoritarian leaders often see themselves as the source of power and authority.

    3. The democratic leader often perceives the group as the source of authority and power.

    4. Supervisors tend to do better when using the pattern of leadership that is most natural for them.

    5. Social scientists suggest that the effective supervisor use the leadership style that best fits the problem or circumstances involved.

    6. All four styles -- telling, selling, consulting, joining -- have their place. Using one does not preclude using the other at another time.

    7. The theory X point of view assumes that the average person dislikes work, will avoid it whenever possible, and must be coerced to achieve organizational objectives.

    8. The theory Y point of view assumes that the average person considers work to be as natural as play, and, when the individual is committed, he requires little supervision or direction to accomplish desired objectives.

    9. The leader's basic assumptions concerning human behavior and human nature affect his actions, decisions, and other managerial practices.

    10. Dissatisfaction among employees is often present, but difficult to isolate. The supervisor should seek to weaken dissatisfaction by keeping promises, being sincere and considerate, keeping employees informed, and so forth.

    11. Constructive suggestions should be encouraged during the natural progress of the work.

V. PROCESSES FOR SOLVING PROBLEMS

    1. People find their daily tasks more meaningful and satisfying when they can improve them.

    2. The causes of problems, or the key factors, are often hidden in the background. Ability to solve problems often involves the ability to isolate them from their backgrounds. There is some substance to the cliché that some persons "can't see the forest for the trees."

    3. New procedures are often developed from old ones. Problems should be broken down into manageable parts. New ideas can be adapted from old ones.

4. People think differently in problem-solving situations. Using a logical, patterned approach is often useful. One approach found to be useful includes these steps:

(a) Define the problem   (d) Weigh and decide
(b) Establish objectives   (e) Take action
(c) Get the facts   (f) Evaluate action

VI. TRAINING FOR RESULTS

1. Participants respond best when they feel training is important to them.
2. The supervisor has responsibility for the training and development of those who report to him.
3. When training is delegated to others, great care must be exercised to insure the trainer has knowledge, aptitude, and interest for his work as a trainer.
4. Training (learning) of some type goes on continually. The most successful supervisor makes certain the learning contributes in a productive manner to operational goals.
5. New employees are particularly susceptible to training. Older employees facing new job situations require specific training, as well as having need for development and growth opportunities.
6. Training needs require continuous monitoring.
7. The training officer of an agency is a professional with a responsibility to assist supervisors in solving training problems.
8. Many of the self-development steps important to the supervisor's own growth are equally important to the development of peers and subordinates. Knowledge of these is important when the supervisor consults with others on development and growth opportunities.

VII. HEALTH, SAFETY, AND ACCIDENT PREVENTION

1. Management-minded supervisors take appropriate measures to assist employees in maintaining health and in assuring safe practices in the work environment.
2. Effective safety training and practices help to avoid injury and accidents.
3. Safety should be a management goal. All infractions of safety which are observed should be corrected without exception.
4. Employees' safety attitude, training and instruction, provision of safe tools and equipment, supervision, and leadership are considered highly important factors which contribute to safety and which can be influenced directly by supervisors.
5. When accidents do occur they should be investigated promptly for very important reasons, including the fact that information which is gained can be used to prevent accidents in the future.

VIII. EQUAL EMPLOYMENT OPPORTUNITY

1. The supervisor should endeavor to treat all employees fairly, without regard to religion, race, sex, or national origin.
2. Groups tend to reflect the attitude of the leader. Prejudice can be detected even in very subtle form. Supervisors must strive to create a feeling of mutual respect and confidence in every employee.
3. Complete utilization of all human resources is a national goal. Equitable consideration should be accorded women in the work force, minority-group members, the physically and mentally handicapped, and the older employee. The important question is: "Who can do the job?"
4. Training opportunities, recognition for performance, overtime assignments, promotional opportunities, and all other personnel actions are to be handled on an equitable basis.

IX. IMPROVING COMMUNICATIONS

1. Communications is achieving understanding between the sender and the receiver of a message. It also means sharing information -- the creation of understanding.
2. Communication is basic to all human activity. Words are means of conveying meanings; however, real meanings are in people.
3. There are very practical differences in the effectiveness of one-way, impersonal, and two-way communications. Words spoken face-to-face are better understood. Telephone conversations are effective, but lack the rapport of person-to-person exchanges. The whole person communicates.
4. Cooperation and communication in an organization go hand in hand. When there is a mutual respect between people, spelling out rules and procedures for communicating is unnecessary.
5. There are several barriers to effective communications. These include failure to listen with respect and understanding, lack of skill in feedback, and misinterpreting the meanings of words used by the speaker. It is also common practice to listen to what we want to hear, and tune out things we do not want to hear.
6. Communication is management's chief problem. The supervisor should accept the challenge to communicate more effectively and to improve interagency and intra-agency communications.
7. The supervisor may often plan for and conduct meetings. The planning phase is critical and may determine the success or the failure of a meeting.
8. Speaking before groups usually requires extra effort. Stage fright may never disappear completely, but it can be controlled.

X. SELF-DEVELOPMENT

1. Every employee is responsible for his own self-development.
2. Toastmaster and toastmistress clubs offer opportunities to improve skills in oral communications.
3. Planning for one's own self-development is of vital importance. Supervisors know their own strengths and limitations better than anyone else.
4. Many opportunities are open to aid the supervisor in his developmental efforts, including job assignments; training opportunities, both governmental and non-governmental -- to include universities and professional conferences and seminars.
5. Programmed instruction offers a means of studying at one's own rate.
6. Where difficulties may arise from a supervisor's being away from his work for training, he may participate in televised home study or correspondence courses to meet his self-develop- ment needs.

XI. TEACHING AND TRAINING

A. The Teaching Process

Teaching is encouraging and guiding the learning activities of students toward established goals. In most cases this process consists in five steps: preparation, presentation, summarization, evaluation, and application.

1. Preparation
Preparation is twofold in nature; that of the supervisor and the employee.
Preparation by the supervisor is absolutely essential to success. He must know what, when, where, how, and whom he will teach. Some of the factors that should be considered are:

(1) The objectives	(5) Employee interest
(2) The materials needed	(6) Training aids
(3) The methods to be used	(7) Evaluation
(4) Employee participation	(8) Summarization

Employee preparation consists in preparing the employee to receive the material. Probably the most important single factor in the preparation of the employee is arousing and maintaining his interest. He must know the objectives of the training, why he is there, how the material can be used, and its importance to him.

2. Presentation

In presentation, have a carefully designed plan and follow it.
The plan should be accurate and complete, yet flexible enough to meet situations as they arise. The method of presentation will be determined by the particular situation and objectives.

3. Summary

A summary should be made at the end of every training unit and program. In addition, there may be internal summaries depending on the nature of the material being taught. The important thing is that the trainee must always be able to understand how each part of the new material relates to the whole.

4. Application

The supervisor must arrange work so the employee will be given a chance to apply new knowledge or skills while the material is still clear in his mind and interest is high. The trainee does not really know whether he has learned the material until he has been given a chance to apply it. If the material is not applied, it loses most of its value.

5. Evaluation

The purpose of all training is to promote learning. To determine whether the training has been a success or failure, the supervisor must evaluate this learning.

In the broadest sense evaluation includes all the devices, methods, skills, and techniques used by the supervisor to keep him self and the employees informed as to their progress toward the objectives they are pursuing. The extent to which the employee has mastered the knowledge, skills, and abilities, or changed his attitudes, as determined by the program objectives, is the extent to which instruction has succeeded or failed.

Evaluation should not be confined to the end of the lesson, day, or program but should be used continuously. We shall note later the way this relates to the rest of the teaching process.

B. Teaching Methods

A teaching method is a pattern of identifiable student and instructor activity used in presenting training material.

All supervisors are faced with the problem of deciding which method should be used at a given time.

As with all methods, there are certain advantages and disadvantages to each method.

1. Lecture

The lecture is direct oral presentation of material by the supervisor. The present trend is to place less emphasis on the trainer's activity and more on that of the trainee.

2. Discussion

Teaching by discussion or conference involves using questions and other techniques to arouse interest and focus attention upon certain areas, and by doing so creating a learning situation. This can be one of the most valuable methods because it gives the employees 'an opportunity to express their ideas and pool their knowledge.

3. Demonstration

 The demonstration is used to teach how something works or how to do something. It can be used to show a principle or what the results of a series of actions will be. A well-staged demonstration is particularly effective because it shows proper methods of performance in a realistic manner.

4. Performance

 Performance is one of the most fundamental of all learning techniques or teaching methods. The trainee may be able to tell how a specific operation should be performed but he cannot be sure he knows how to perform the operation until he has done so.

5. Which Method to Use

 Moreover, there are other methods and techniques of teaching. It is difficult to use any method without other methods entering into it. In any learning situation a combination of methods is usually more effective than anyone method alone.

 Finally, evaluation must be integrated into the other aspects of the teaching-learning process.
 It must be used in the motivation of the trainees; it must be used to assist in developing understanding during the training; and it must be related to employee application of the results of training.
 This is distinctly the role of the supervisor.

ANSWER SHEET

TEST NO. _____ PART _____ TITLE OF POSITION _____

(AS GIVEN IN EXAMINATION ANNOUNCEMENT - INCLUDE OPTION, IF ANY)

PLACE OF EXAMINATION _____ DATE _____

(CITY OR TOWN) (STATE)

RATING
....

USE THE SPECIAL PENCIL.   MAKE GLOSSY BLACK MARKS.

1 2 3 4 5 6 7 8 9 10 (A B C D E)
26 27 28 29 30 31 32 33 34 35 (A B C D E)
51 52 53 54 55 56 57 58 59 60 (A B C D E)
76 77 78 79 80 81 82 83 84 85 (A B C D E)
101 102 103 104 105 106 107 108 109 110 (A B C D E)

Make only ONE mark for each answer.   Additional and stray marks may be
counted as mistakes.   In making corrections, erase errors COMPLETELY.

11 12 13 14 15 16 17 18 19 20 21 22 23 24 25 (A B C D E)
36 37 38 39 40 41 42 43 44 45 46 47 48 49 50 (A B C D E)
61 62 63 64 65 66 67 68 69 70 71 72 73 74 75 (A B C D E)
86 87 88 89 90 91 92 93 94 95 96 97 98 99 100 (A B C D E)
111 112 113 114 115 116 117 118 119 120 121 122 123 124 125 (A B C D E)

ANSWER SHEET

TEST NO. ____________ PART ______ TITLE OF POSITION ______________________________
(AS GIVEN IN EXAMINATION ANNOUNCEMENT - INCLUDE OPTION, IF ANY)

PLACE OF EXAMINATION ______________________________ (CITY OR TOWN) ______________ (STATE) DATE ______________

RATING

USE THE SPECIAL PENCIL. MAKE GLOSSY BLACK MARKS.

1	A B C D E	26	A B C D E	51	A B C D E	76	A B C D E	101	A B C D E
2	A B C D E	27	A B C D E	52	A B C D E	77	A B C D E	102	A B C D E
3	A B C D E	28	A B C D E	53	A B C D E	78	A B C D E	103	A B C D E
4	A B C D E	29	A B C D E	54	A B C D E	79	A B C D E	104	A B C D E
5	A B C D E	30	A B C D E	55	A B C D E	80	A B C D E	105	A B C D E
6	A B C D E	31	A B C D E	56	A B C D E	81	A B C D E	106	A B C D E
7	A B C D E	32	A B C D E	57	A B C D E	82	A B C D E	107	A B C D E
8	A B C D E	33	A B C D E	58	A B C D E	83	A B C D E	108	A B C D E
9	A B C D E	34	A B C D E	59	A B C D E	84	A B C D E	109	A B C D E
10	A B C D E	35	A B C D E	60	A B C D E	85	A B C D E	110	A B C D E

Make only ONE mark for each answer. Additional and stray marks may be counted as mistakes. In making corrections, erase errors COMPLETELY.

11	A B C D E	36	A B C D E	61	A B C D E	86	A B C D E	111	A B C D E
12	A B C D E	37	A B C D E	62	A B C D E	87	A B C D E	112	A B C D E
13	A B C D E	38	A B C D E	63	A B C D E	88	A B C D E	113	A B C D E
14	A B C D E	39	A B C D E	64	A B C D E	89	A B C D E	114	A B C D E
15	A B C D E	40	A B C D E	65	A B C D E	90	A B C D E	115	A B C D E
16	A B C D E	41	A B C D E	66	A B C D E	91	A B C D E	116	A B C D E
17	A B C D E	42	A B C D E	67	A B C D E	92	A B C D E	117	A B C D E
18	A B C D E	43	A B C D E	68	A B C D E	93	A B C D E	118	A B C D E
19	A B C D E	44	A B C D E	69	A B C D E	94	A B C D E	119	A B C D E
20	A B C D E	45	A B C D E	70	A B C D E	95	A B C D E	120	A B C D E
21	A B C D E	46	A B C D E	71	A B C D E	96	A B C D E	121	A B C D E
22	A B C D E	47	A B C D E	72	A B C D E	97	A B C D E	122	A B C D E
23	A B C D E	48	A B C D E	73	A B C D E	98	A B C D E	123	A B C D E
24	A B C D E	49	A B C D E	74	A B C D E	99	A B C D E	124	A B C D E
25	A B C D E	50	A B C D E	75	A B C D E	100	A B C D E	125	A B C D E